130 New Iris Folded Cards to Make

Maruscha Gaasenbeek

Search Press

Imprint

First published in Great Britain 2011 by Search Press Limited, Wellwood, North Farm Road, Tunbridge Wells, Kent TN2 3DR

Chapters 1 and 2 originally published in The Netherlands by Forte Uitgevers, Utrecht as Iris Folding for Fun © 2007 and Iris Folding with Love © 2006

Copyright © 2011 Forte Uitgevers, Utrecht

English edition produced by GreenGate Publishing Services

ISBN: 978-1-84448-610-6

Suppliers
If you have any difficulty in obtaining any of the materials and equipment mentioned in this book, please visit the Search Press website for details of suppliers: www.searchpress.com

Although every attempt has been made to ensure that all the materials and equipment used in this book are currently available, the Publishers cannot guarantee that this will always be the case. If you have difficulty in obtaining any of the items mentioned, then suitable alternatives should be used instead.

Contents

Chapter 2

Iris Folding with Love 39

Chapter 3

Iris Folding: a Full Year 69

Preface

Welcome to *130 New Iris Folded Cards to Make*. This compendium is made up of three books, *Iris Folding for Fun*, *Iris Folding with Love* and *Iris Folding: a Full Year*.

Iris folding is a simple technique that has found its way all over the world; just cut out the pattern, cut off strips of paper in different colours, put them in the right place and a unique card is born. Card makers often use the patterned and coloured inner side of envelopes; wrapping paper is also a popular choice and, especially in the USA, origami paper is used. The most important thing is that you can fold the paper easily and that you have a wide variety of colours and patterns at your disposal. In this way, you can experiment with the designs and create your own unique combinations.

Put simply, iris folding involves drawing a pattern, converting the shape to a basic template and covering this with regularly changing sections. However, there is an art to designing the pattern correctly and to positioning the 'pupil', the centre, exactly where you want it, and it can help if you are able to do this mathematically. You can then play around with colours, from dazzling brights to softer tints and anything in between, as long as there is an obvious colour contrast to draw attention to the rotation in the iris.

There are many possibilities for using iris folding to make your own greetings cards, decorate a scrapbook or make a decoration to hang on the wall.

I hope you enjoy making all the patterns in this book, and find inspiration and ideas for designing many more of your own.

Chapter 1: Iris Folding for Fun

Techniques

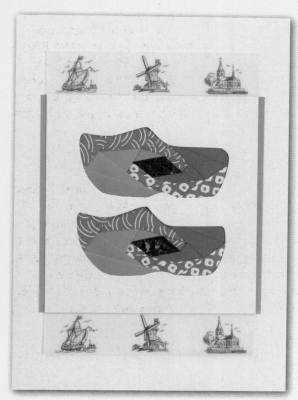

The starting point with any iris folding is the pattern. You begin by cutting the outer shape of the pattern from the back of your card and subsequently building the pattern inwards with folded paper strips. You work on the back of your window – in mirror image – and then finally place your work on another piece of card. For a square pattern you could, for example, choose four different-coloured or patterned papers that harmonise and contrast well. Trim or cut the paper into strips in the same direction: for example, from right to left. The total number of strips per colour in a pattern is between three and six. These can be cut from one strip of 15 × 1.5cm (6 × ½in) per colour. You then fold over the edge of each strip and place them into separate piles. Cover section after section of the design by following the numerical order (1, 2, 3, 4, 5, etc.) and alternating the colours. Place the strips with the fold facing towards the centre of the pattern and attach them left to right on to the card with tape. Finally, cover the centre with an eye-catching piece of holographic paper.

The basic pattern

(see page 12 bottom right and card 1 page 15)
It is important to start with the basic matruska pattern, as this teaches you the unique way of folding and fixing that you will need for all patterns. You will notice that you will quickly become familiar with the techniques of iris folding.

Preparation

1 Place the white card measuring 8.5 × 6.5cm (3¼ × 2½in) with the back towards you.
2 Use a pencil to draw the outline of the matruska on your card with the help of a light box and cut out the pattern.
3 Tape a copy of the matruska pattern (page 14) from this book on to your cutting mat.
4 Place the card with the hole exactly over the pattern (again you are facing the back of the card) and secure it to your cutting mat with a few pieces of masking tape on the left-hand side.
5 Choose four sheets of paper with different designs. For the card on page 12 bottom right, four different designs have been used in origami red.
6 Cut these into strips of 1.5cm (½in) wide and make separate piles of colour A, colour B, colour C and colour D.
7 Fold a border lengthwise along each strip with the patterned side outwards.

Iris folding

8 Take a folded strip of colour A and place it pattern-side down over section 1 against the line of the pattern with the folded edge towards the middle. Allow 0.5cm (¼in) of the strips to extend either side and trim the excess. The strip at the bottom should also slightly overlap the edge of the pattern so that section 1 is totally covered.

9 Attach the left- and right-hand sides of the strip to the card with a small piece of tape, 0.5cm (¼in) from the card's edge.
10 Take colour B and place the strip on section 2 of the pattern. Again attach it on the left and the right.
11 Take colour C and attach to section 3.
12 Take colour D and attach to section 4.
13 Continue with colour A on section 5, colour B on 6, colour C on 7 and colour D on 8.

NB There is no section 17 so that particular strip of colour A is cancelled. Continue with colour B on section 18. The strips on sections 1, 5, 9 and 13 of this pattern all have colour A. The strips on 2, 6, 10, 14 and 18 all have colour B, the strips on 3, 7, 11, 15 and 19 are colour C and the strips on 4, 8, 12, 16 and the little dot 20 are colour D.

Finishing

Having completed section 20, remove the card. Tape a piece of holographic paper over the centre on the back. To finish the card you can use punching, decorative papers and cut outs. Attach double-sided tape along the edges or use 3D foam tape to create extra thickness. Remove the protective layer and attach your work on to double card. Do not use glue as the paper strips place pressure on the card.

Step-by-step

1. Start with a range of papers in all the colours of the rainbow!

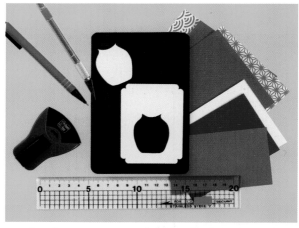

2. Cut the pattern out of the back of single card.

3. Fix the folded strips in numerical order on to the back of the card.

4. Turn the card over from time to time to check that the design is developing nicely.

Materials

To make the cards:

- ❒ card, for example Canson Mi-Teintes (C), cArt-us (cA), Papicolor (P)
- ❒ cutting knife, cutting mat
- ❒ ruler with a metal cutting edge (e.g. Securit)
- ❒ adhesive tape
- ❒ double-sided adhesive tape
- ❒ 3D foam tape
- ❒ masking tape
- ❒ corner punches and punches (e.g. MakeMe!, Fiskars, Carl)
- ❒ pair of scissors and silhouette scissors
- ❒ corner scissors (e.g. Fiskars)
- ❒ hole punch
- ❒ tweezers
- ❒ fine-liner pen, black
- ❒ photo glue
- ❒ light box

Iris folding

Strips of:

- ❒ used envelopes
- ❒ iris folding paper (IF paper)
- ❒ single-sided and double-sided (hereafter s.s. and d.s.) origami paper
- ❒ craft papers

The centre:

- ❒ holographic paper

The patterns

The patterns for all the cards in this book are shown as actual size. Draw the outline using a light box. You can easily cut out the patterns from card with a sharp knife or with silhouette scissors. Use the hole punch for rings and circles and the fine-liner pen for all drawings.

Red

For all the cards follow the basic techniques (pages 10 to 12).

Card 1

- Card: 8 × 16cm (3¼ × 6¼in) and 8.5 × 6.5cm (3¼ × 2½in) white, 10.5 × 7cm (4¼ × 2¾in) Christmas red P43, 10.5 × 6.5cm (4¼ × 2½in) bright red C506
- Matruska pattern
- 1.5cm (½in) wide strips of four different origami papers in red
- 3 × 3cm (1¼ × 1¼in) origami paper in red for hair and soft pink for face
- Holographic paper (rainbow)
- Corner punch (accolade)

Card 2

- Card: 9 × 18cm (3½ × 7in) cerise P33, 7 × 7cm (2¾ × 2¾in) Christmas red, 6.5 × 6.5cm (2½ × 2½in) bronze P164
- Apple pattern (page 23)
- 1.5cm (½in) wide strips of four different red envelopes
- Holographic paper (soft red)

Card 3

- Card: 10.5 × 15cm (4¼ × 6in) wine red P36, 7.5 × 5.8cm (3 × 2¼in) blossom P34
- Paper: 9 × 6.3cm (3½ × 2½in) red origami paper
- Christmas ball pattern (page 30)
- 1.5cm (½in) wide strips of three origami papers in red
- Holographic paper (red)

See page 30.

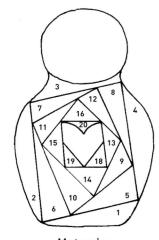

Matruska

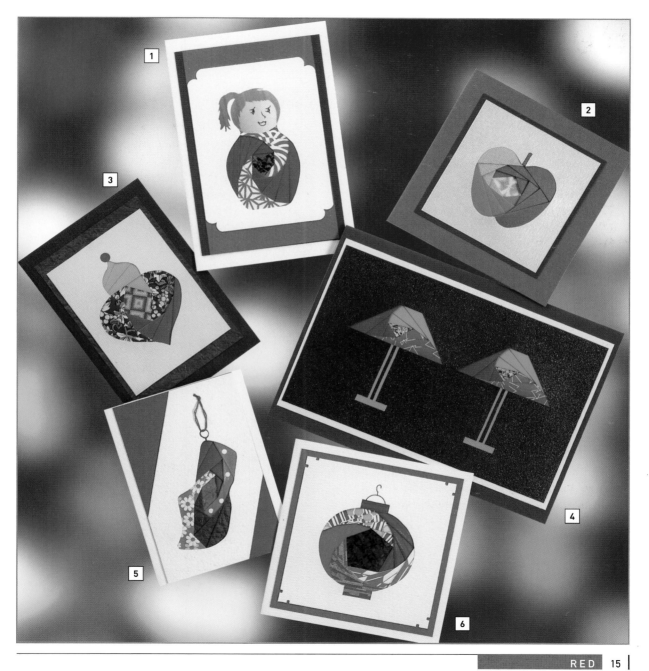

Card 4

- Card: 21 × 14.8cm (8¼ × 5¾in) purple P604, 9.2 × 14.5cm (3½ × 5¾in) light pink C103, 8.5 × 14cm (3¼ × 5½in) aubergine P146
- Lamp pattern (page 20)
- 1.5cm (½in) wide strips of two origami papers in red and one IF paper in dark red
- Holographic paper (copper)

Cut the shade twice out of the smallest card. Cut out the stand and base from light pink paper and attach.

Card 5

- Card: 9.5 × 14cm (3¾ × 5½in) and 6 × 9.5cm (2¼ × 3¾in) white, 6 × 9.5cm (2¼ × 3¾in) fiesta red P12
- Clog pattern (page 34)
- 1.5cm (½in) wide strips of three red origami papers and one red envelope
- Holographic paper (red)
- Cotton red

Slant the small white card with two triangles: top left 5.8 × 3cm (2¼ × 1¼in) and bottom right 2 × 4cm (¾ × 1½in). Turn the card over, draw and cut the clog out of the back.

Card 6

- Card: 9 × 18cm (3½ × 7in) and 7.5 × 7.5cm (3 × 3in) white, 8.2 × 8.2cm (3¼ × 3¼in) fiesta red P12
- Chinese lantern pattern (page 35)
- 1.5cm (½in) wide strips of two red envelopes and three red origami papers
- Holographic paper (rainbow)
- Corner punch (spear)

Pink

Card 1

- Card: 18 × 14.8cm (7 × 5¾in) warm pink cA485, 8 × 14cm (3¼ × 5½in) apricot P24, 2 × 13.5cm (¾ × 5¼in) cerise P33, 6.5 × 13.5cm (2½ × 5¼in) soft pink cA480
- Hedgehog pattern
- 1.5cm (½in) wide strips of eight pink origami papers
- Holographic paper (pink)

Use a pencil to trace the hedgehogs on to the back of the soft pink card and also a mirror image, including spines and paws. Draw the spines and paws at the front using a fine-liner pen. Cut the top corners of the soft pink card round and cut out both hedgehogs. Draw the eyes and nose after the iris folding. Fix the cerise strip underneath, then on to apricot card and finally on to double card.

Card 2

- Card: 10.5 × 21cm (4¼ × 8¼in) bright pink P606, 8 × 8cm (3¼ × 3¼in) pink P605
- Chinese lantern pattern (page 35)
- 1.5cm (½in) wide strips of five pink origami papers
- Holographic paper (pink)

For A and B, use colour C.

Card 3

- Card: 14.8 × 21cm (5¾ × 8¼in) pink P605, 14.8 × 8.8cm (5¾ × 3½in) mirror pink, 14.8 × 7cm (5¾ × 2¾in) light pink C103
- Mirror pattern (page 29)
- 1.5cm (½in) wide strips of four pink origami papers
- Mirror paper (pink) P123

See Turquoise, card 1.

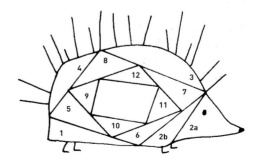

Hedgehog

Card 4

- Card: 10 × 20cm (4 × 7¾in) pink P184, 6 × 8cm (2¼ × 3¼in) blossom
- Piggy bank pattern (page 32)
- 1.5cm (½in) wide strips of four pink origami papers (e.g. Japanese design, d.s. plain, d.s. stripe, d.s. pearly white)
- Holographic paper (rainbow)

See Blue, card 1.

Card 5

- Card: 7.5 × 15cm (3 × 6in) cerise P33, 5 × 5cm (2 × 2in) white
- Jewel pattern
- 1.5cm (½in) wide strips of two craft papers with pink blossom design and two origami papers in pink

Cut the jewel out of the white card. Draw an eyelet after the iris folding.

Card 6

- Card: 8 × 16cm (3¼ × 6¼in) dark rose pink, 10.3 × 7.5cm (4 × 3in) pale blossom pink, 9.5 × 7cm (3¾ × 2¾in) mid pink P605
- Matruska pattern (page 14)
- 1.5cm (½in) wide strips of three pink origami papers and one paper cake case
- 3 × 3cm (1¼ × 1¼in) origami paper in pink for hat and soft pink for face
- Holographic paper (pearly white)
- Corner scissors (nostalgia)

Note: no section 17, no strip of colour A.

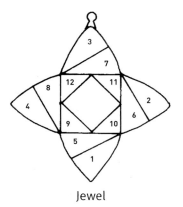

Jewel

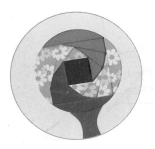

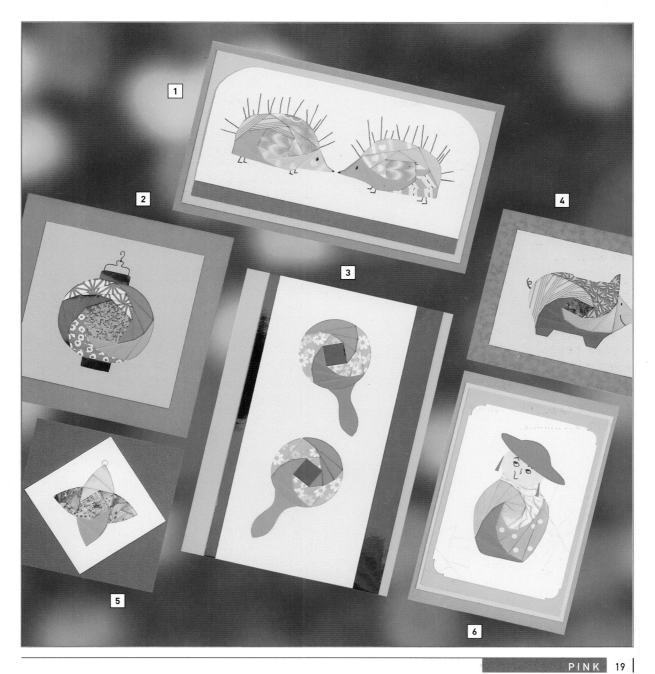

Orange

Card 1

- Card: 8 × 16cm (3¼ × 6¼in) dark orange P608, 7 × 7cm (2¾ × 2¾in) white
- IF paper 7.4 × 7.4cm (3 × 3in) bronze
- Lamp pattern
- 1.5cm (½in) wide strips of three IF papers in orange/bronze
- Holographic paper (bronze)

Cut out only the shade from the white card and cover with the strips. Copy the stand and base on to orange paper, cut out and attach.

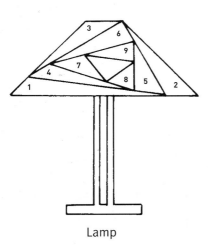

Lamp

Card 2

- Card: 16 × 12cm (6¼ × 4¾in) and 5.5 × 8cm (2¼ × 3¼in) off-white P612, 6 × 8cm (2¼ × 3¼in) light orange P609
- Hedgehog pattern (page 17)
- 1.5cm (½in) wide strips of three origami papers in light orange and leaf design and one in bronze P110
- Holographic paper (orange)
- Leaves from corner punch

Omit the paws and draw the eye and spines in sleeping position.

Card 3

- Card: 12.5 × 25cm (5 × 9¾in) and 1 × 4cm (½ × 1½in) rust P186, 8.8 × 8.8cm (3½ × 3½in) glossy orange, 7 × 7cm (2¾ × 2¾in) ivory white
- Orange craft paper, 9.5 × 9.5cm (3¾ × 3¾in)
- Chinese lantern pattern (page 35)
- 1.5cm (½in) wide strips of five orange origami papers
- Holographic paper (bronze)

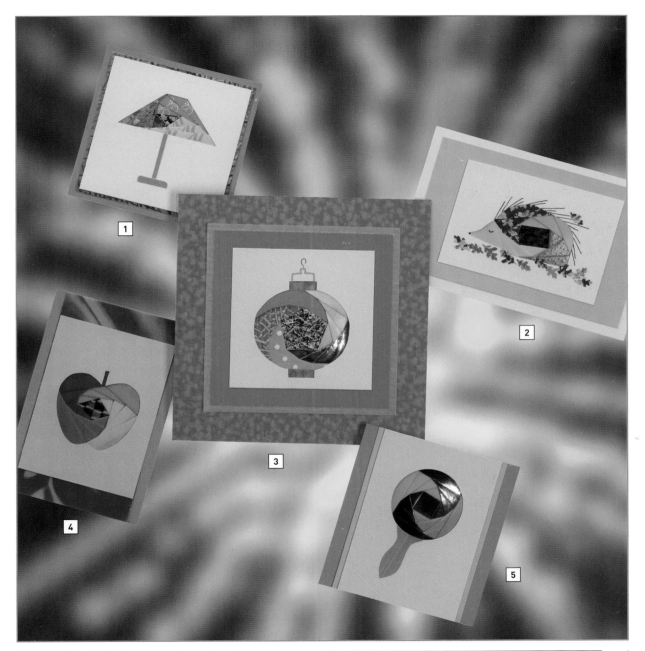

Card 4

- Card: 10.5 × 14cm (4¼ × 5½in) orange P608, 8 × 6cm (3¼ × 2¼in) light orange P609
- Vellum: 10.5 × 6cm (4¼ × 2¼in) ivory satin
- Apple pattern (page 23)
- 1.5cm (½in) wide strips of four orange origami papers

Card 5

- Card: 8.5 × 16cm (3¼ × 6¼in) orange, 8.5 × 6.5cm (3¼ × 2½in) mango, 8.5 × 6cm (3¼ × 2¼in) light mango
- Mirror pattern (page 29)
- 1.5cm (½in) wide strips of four orange origami papers

Card with clogs on page 8

- Card: 14.8 × 21cm (5¾ × 8¼in) and 8.5 × 8cm (3¼ × 3¼in) white
- Clog pattern (page 34)
- Paper: 8.5 × 8.5cm (3¼ × 3¼in) origami in orange and two strips of 2 × 8cm (¾ × 3¼in) traditional Dutch tile design
- 1.5cm (½in) wide strips of four orange origami papers
- Holographic paper (orange)

Attach the clogs to the sheet of orange origami paper after the iris folding. Attach the strips with the tile design on the top and bottom and attach everything on to double white card.

Yellow

Card 1

- Card: 8 × 16cm (3¼ × 6¼in) mustard yellow P48, 6.5 × 6.5cm (2½ × 2½in) white
- Apple pattern
- 1.5cm (½in) wide strips of four origami papers (rainbow colour)
- Holographic paper (gold)

Cut the apple out of the white card. Cut the strips, separate the colours, cover the apple and finish off with the holographic 'pips'. Attach everything to double yellow card.

Card 2

- Card: 21 × 14.8cm (8¼ × 5¾in) fruity orange P135, 4 × 14.8cm (1½ × 5¾in) soft yellow P611, 4 × 14.8cm (1½ × 5¾in) yellow P610, 6 × 14.8cm (1½ × 2¼in) white
- Clog pattern (page 34)
- 1.5cm (½in) wide strips of four yellow origami papers
- Holographic paper (yellow)

Card 3

- Card: 16 × 12cm (6¼ × 4¾in) soft yellow P611, 7 × 10.5cm (2¾ × 4¼in) nut brown P39, 6.5 × 9cm (2½ × 3½in) soft yellow P132
- Hedgehog pattern (page 17)
- 1.5cm (½in) wide strips of four yellow and brown envelopes
- Holographic paper (gold)
- 3-in-1 corner punch (leaves)

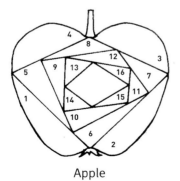

Apple

Card 4

- Card: 12.5 × 16cm (5 × 6¼in) mustard yellow P48, 11 × 7.5cm (4¼ × 3in) buttercup yellow P10, 11 × 6.5cm (4¼ × 2½in) white
- Vase pattern (page 28)
- 1.5cm (½in) wide strips of two yellow origami papers and two IF papers in gold-yellow
- Holographic paper (gold)
- Flowers from different punches

Note: no sections 5 and 7.

Card 5

- Card: 12.5 × 25cm (5 × 9¾in) sunflower P134, 9 × 9cm (3½ × 3½in) soft yellow P132
- Paper: 10 × 10cm (4 × 4in) holographic gold with star
- Chinese lantern pattern (page 35)
- 1.5cm (½in) wide strips of three yellow envelopes and two origami papers in gold
- 1 × 5cm (½ × 2in) black paper for A and B
- Holographic paper (gold)
- Punch (Asian sign)

Use half of the punch design on the corners of the smallest card.

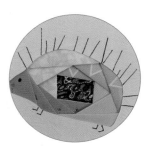

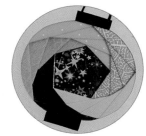

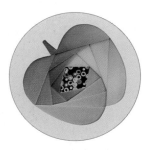

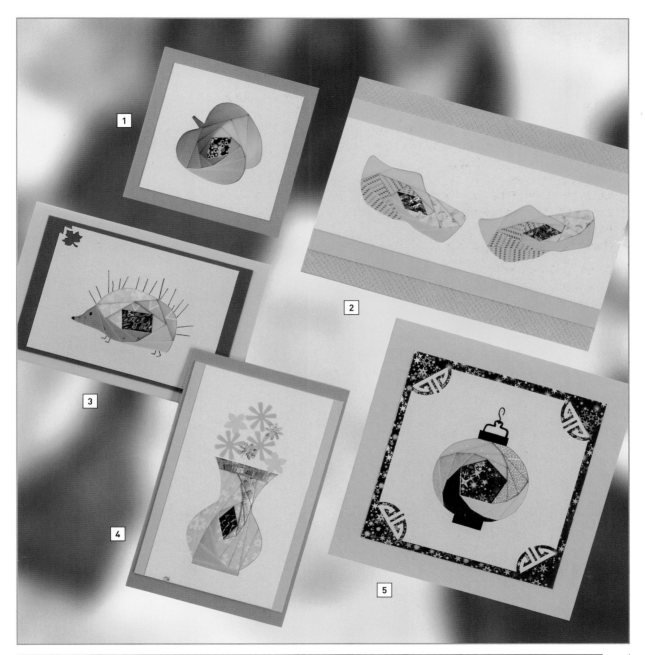

Green

Card 1

- Card: 13 × 13cm (5 × 5in) grass green P07, 12 × 12cm (4¾ × 4¾in) white
- Paper: 12.5 × 12.5cm (5 × 5in) lime envelope
- Vase pattern (page 28)
- 1.5cm (½in) wide strips of four green envelopes
- 7 × 10cm (2¾ × 4in) lime and green envelopes for leaf
- Holographic paper (gold)

Cut the vase out of the white card. Note: sections 5 and 7 of the iris folding are missing, so skip colour A and colour C in that round. Place two envelopes on top of each other with the colour side facing inwards and cut out the leaf design in one go. Attach these above the vase. Attach the white card to the lime sheet and then to the green card.

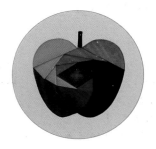

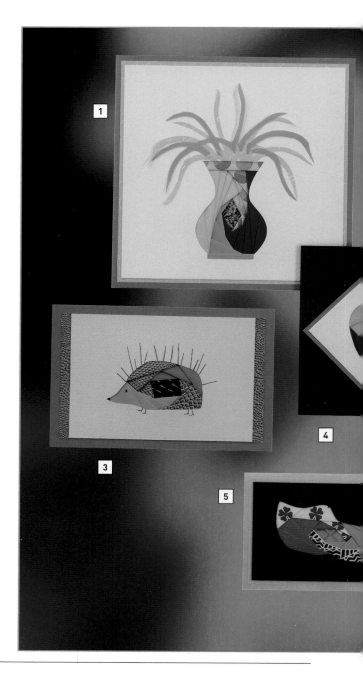

Card 2

- Card: 12.5 × 25cm (5 × 9¾in) and 7 × 7cm (2¾ × 2¾in) fresh green P130, 10.6 × 10.6cm (4¼ × 4¼in) grass green P07, 10 × 10cm (4 × 4in) olive green P45
- Chinese lantern pattern (page 35)
- 1.5cm (½in) wide strips of five green origami papers
- Holographic paper (gold)
- Corner punch (spear)

Card 3

- Card: 16 × 12cm (6¼ × 4¾in) grass green P07, 7 × 10cm (2¾ × 4in) lime green
- Paper: 7 × 11cm (2¾ × 4¼in) green snake-skin design P304
- Hedgehog pattern (page 17)
- 1.5cm (½in) wide strips of two green envelopes and two in green snake-skin design P304
- Holographic paper (green)

Card 4

- Card: 9.5 × 17cm (3¾ × 6¾in) Christmas green P18, 6.4 × 6.4cm (2½ × 2½in) grass green P07, 6 × 6cm (2¼ × 2¼in) white
- Apple pattern (page 23)
- 1.5cm (½in) wide strips of four origami papers in green and red
- Holographic paper (green)

Card 5

- Card: 13 × 9cm (5 × 3½in) mint P138, 5.8 × 8cm (2¼ × 3¼in) Christmas green P18
- 6 × 8.5cm (2¼ × 3¼in) transparent paper in kiwi P149
- Clog pattern (page 34)
- 1.5cm (½in) wide strips of design paper in waffle green, two green envelopes and one green origami paper
- Holographic paper (green)

Card 6

- Card: 14.8 × 21cm (5¾ × 8¼in) light green P624, 10.4 × 7.7cm (4 × 3in) green P623, 9 × 6.5cm (3½ × 2½in) white
- 10.8 × 8.2cm (4¼ × 3¼in) origami paper in green
- Matruska pattern (page 14)
- 1.5cm (½in) wide strips of four green origami papers
- 3 × 3cm (1¼ × 1¼in) green origami paper for hair and soft green for face
- Holographic paper (green)
- Corner scissors (nostalgia)

Note: no section 17.

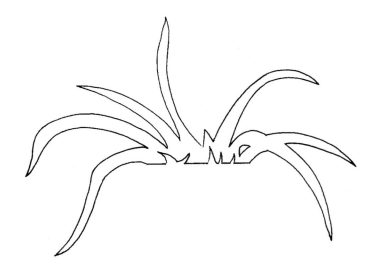

Vase

Turquoise

Card 1

- Card: 10.5 × 21cm (4¼ × 8¼in) mint cA331, 9.4 × 9cm (3¾ × 3½in) blue-green, 7.4 × 7cm (3 × 2¾in) white
- Mirror pattern
- 1.5cm (½in) wide strips of four green envelopes
- Mirror paper (silver)

Cut a circle of diameter 3.6cm (1½in) from the white card and fill with the strips. Trace the handle and glue it to the edge of the circle. Glue the white card diagonally on to blue-green card and then on to double card.

Card 2

- Card: 12 × 20cm (4¾ × 7¾in) turquoise, 9 × 7cm (3½ × 2¾in) white P108
- Paper: 11.4 × 9.5cm (4½ × 3¾in) turquoise with leaf pattern
- Lamp pattern (page 20)
- 1.5cm (½in) wide strips of three origami papers in blue-green
- Holographic paper (blue-green)

Card 3

- Card: 13 × 10cm (5 × 4in) turquoise, 5.5 × 9cm (2¼ × 3½in) mint
- Clog pattern (page 34)
- 1.5cm (½in) wide strips of four green envelopes
- Holographic paper (turquoise)

Glue strips of green envelope paper behind the top and bottom of the mint card.

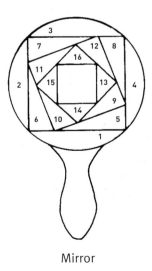

Mirror

Card 4

- Card: 14.8 × 21cm (5¾ × 8¼in) Christmas green P18, 10 × 7.8cm (4 × 3in) dark green P16, 9 × 7cm (3½ × 2¾in) sea green P17
- Paper: 10.7 × 8.5cm (4¼ × 3¼in) green origami paper
- Christmas ball pattern
- 1.5cm (½in) wide strips of four green origami papers
- Holographic paper (silver)

Cut the Christmas ball out of the smallest card. After iris folding, decorate the front with circles cut with the hole punch. Glue the sea green card on to the dark green, the green origami paper and then on to double card.

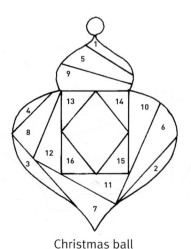

Christmas ball

Card 5

- Card: 7.5 × 15cm (3 × 6in) cornflower blue cA393, 7 × 7cm (2¾ × 2¾in) green cA367, 6.5 × 6.5cm (2½ × 2½in) white
- Jewel pattern (page 18)
- 1.5cm (½in) wide strips of four origami papers in blue-green
- Holographic paper (silver)

Card 6

- Card: 10 × 15cm (4 × 6in) dark petrol, 9.5 × 7.5cm (3¾ × 3in) petrol, 9 × 7cm (3½ × 2¾in) sea green P17
- Vase pattern (page 28)
- 1.5cm (½in) wide strips of four green origami papers
- Holographic paper (rainbow)

Note: no sections 5 and 7.

Blue

Card 1

- Card: 18 × 12cm (7 × 4¾in) royal blue P136, 8 × 10.5cm (3¼ × 4¼in) light blue P619
- Paper: 8.5 × 11.2cm (3¼ × 4½in) Venetian blue craft paper
- Piggy bank pattern
- 1.5cm (½in) wide strips from two craft papers with blue Venetian design and two blue origami papers
- Holographic paper (blue)

Trace the pattern on to the light blue card and draw the tail first. Cut out the pig. Cover with strips. Draw the snout and eye on the front. Glue the card on to the sheet of Venetian blue craft paper and then on to double card.

Card 2

- Card: 13 × 10cm (5 × 4in) royal blue P136, 5.5 × 9cm (2¼ × 3½in) shell white P190
- Clog pattern (page 34)
- 1.5cm (½in) wide strips from two blue envelopes and two blue IF papers
- Holographic paper (blue)

Cut the clog out of the white card. Cover with strips. Glue the card on to double blue card.

Card 3

- Card: 10.5 × 21cm (4¼ × 8¼in) dark blue P621 and 7.5 × 7.5cm (3 × 3in) white P618
- Paper: 8.5 × 8.5cm (3¼ × 3¼in) dark blue envelope and 8 × 8cm (3¼ × 3¼in) holographic silver
- Chinese lantern pattern (page 35)
- 1.5cm (½in) wide strips from five blue envelopes
- Holographic paper (silver)

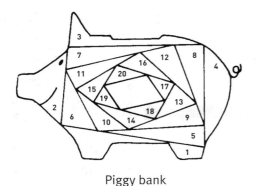

Piggy bank

Card 4

- Card: 10 × 13cm (4 × 5in) champagne P163, 9 × 6cm (3½ × 2¼in) night blue P41
- Mirror pattern (page 29)
- 1.5cm (½in) wide strips from two blue patterned papers and two blue origami papers
- Holographic paper (silver)

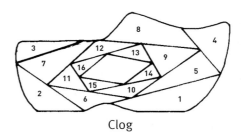

Clog

Card 5

- Card: 14.8 × 21cm (5¾ × 8¼in) ice blue P42, 10.5 × 7.8cm (4¼ × 3in) cornflower blue P05, 9.5 × 7cm (3¾ × 2¾in) dark blue P06 and 9 × 6.5cm (3½ × 2½in) white
- Matruska pattern (page 14)
- 1.5cm (½in) wide strips from four blue origami papers
- 3 × 3cm (1¼ × 1¼in) blue gloss paper for hair and light blue for face
- Holographic paper (silver)

Note: no section 17.

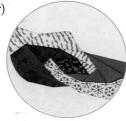

Card 6

- Card: 11 × 16cm (4¼ × 6¼in) night blue P41, 9 × 7cm (3½ × 2¾in) royal blue P136
- Christmas ball pattern (page 30)
- 1.5cm (½in) wide strips from two light blue envelopes and two silver IF papers
- Holographic paper (silver)
- Corner punch (snowflakes)

Punch a corner in the smallest card and cover with holographic paper.

Purple

Card 1

- Card: 12.5 × 25cm (5 × 9¾in) and 6.5 × 6.5cm (2½ × 2½in) pebble P161, 10.3 × 10.3cm (4 × 4in) purple P46, 7.2 × 7.2cm (2¾ × 2¾in) lilac P37, 6.8 × 6.8cm (2¾ × 2¾in) mirror purple P124
- Jewel pattern (page 18)
- 1.5cm (½in) wide strips from four purple origami papers
- Holographic paper (purple)

After the iris folding, glue the three cards in order of size on top of each other. Attach them to the purple card and then straight on to double card.

Card 2

- Card: 10.5 × 21cm (4¼ × 8¼in) and 7.8 × 7.8cm (3 × 3in) purple P601, 8.2 × 8.2cm white, 7.5 × 7.5cm (3 × 3in) lilac P603
- Chinese lantern pattern
- 1.5cm (½in) wide strips from six purple envelopes
- Holographic paper (purple)

Cut the Chinese lantern from the lilac card. Use the same colour for A and B and fill the lantern with the other strips. Cut a hanger and draw a hook. Glue the pieces of card on top of each other.

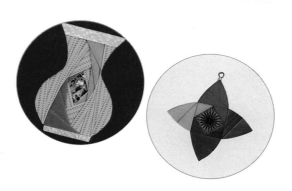

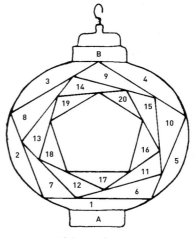

Chinese lantern

Card 3

- Card: 6 × 17cm (2¼ × 6¾in) aubergine P604, 5.5 × 7.5cm (2¼ × 3in) lilac C104
- Piggy bank pattern (page 32)
- 1.5cm (½in) wide strips from four purple envelopes
- Holographic paper (purple)

Card 4

- Card: 12 × 20cm (4¾ × 7¾in) lilac, 7.7 × 5.5cm (3 × 2¼in) purple
- Paper: 11.2 × 9.4cm (4½ × 3¾in) purple with golden flower design, 7.7 × 7cm (3 × 2¾in) cream P109
- Vase pattern (page 28)
- 1.5cm (½in) wide strips from four origami papers in violet and cream P109
- Holographic paper (gold)

Note: no sections 5 and 7.

 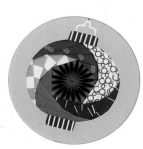

Card 5

- Card: 14.8 × 21cm (5¾ × 8¼in) and 9 × 6.5cm (3½ × 2½in) white, 12.5 × 8cm (5 × 3¼in) violet P14, 12 × 7.5cm (4¾ × 3in) purple P46
- Matruska pattern (page 14)
- 1.5cm (½in) wide strips from three purple origami papers and one purple IF paper
- 3 × 3cm (1¼ × 1¼in) origami paper in purple for hair and violet for face
- Holographic paper (purple)
- Corner punch (accolade)

Note: no section 17.

Card 6

- Card: 12 × 16cm (4¾ × 6¼in) lilac cA453, 10 × 7.3cm (4 × 2¾in) purple, 9 × 6.8cm (3½ × 2¾in) white
- Christmas ball pattern (page 30)
- 1.5cm (½in) wide strips of four purple origami papers
- Holographic paper (silver)
- Corner punch (Christmas)

Punch two corners of the white card and cut out the shape.

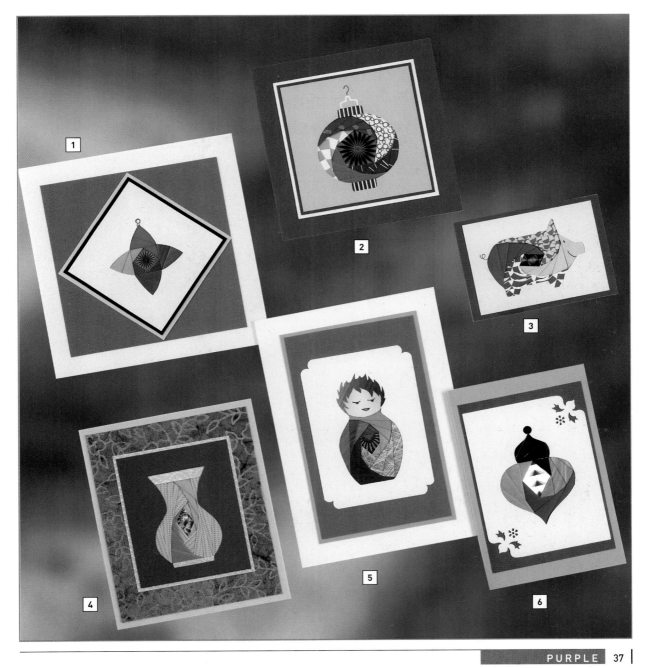

Chapter 2: Iris Folding with Love

Techniques

The starting point for iris folding is the pattern. Cut the outline of the pattern out of the back of your card and then fill the hole from the outside to the inside with strips of folded paper. You work at the back of the card, so you work, in fact, on a mirror image. When you have finished the iris folding, stick the card on to another card. For a triangular pattern, select three different pieces of paper for which the patterns and colours combine or contrast nicely. Cut all the paper into strips in the same way, for example, from left to right. Depending on the pattern, you will need between four and eight strips. The width of the strips also depends on the pattern and is stated in the instructions given for each card. You need to first fold the edge of the strips over and then sort them into the different colours. Next, cover each section in turn by following the numbers (1, 2, 3, 4, 5, etc.) using a different colour each time. Lay the strips down with the fold facing towards the middle of the pattern and stick the left and right-hand sides of the strips to the card using adhesive tape. Finally, use an attractive piece of holographic paper to cover the hole in the middle.

The basic pattern

(see card 1 on page 45 and the step-by-step on page 42)
It is important to start with the basic pattern, because from this, you will learn the unique folding and sticking technique needed for all the patterns. You will notice that you will quickly get used to the technique of iris folding.

Preparation

1 Lay the natural card (12.5 × 7.3cm) (5 × 2¾in) down with the back facing towards you.
2 With the aid of a light box, copy the triangular pattern on to the card using a pencil and cut it out.
3 Stick a copy of the basic pattern given in this chapter (pattern 1 on page 44) to your cutting mat using adhesive tape.
4 Place the card with the hole over the pattern (you should be looking at the back of the card) and only stick the left-hand side of the card to your cutting mat using masking tape.
5 Select three different sheets of paper with different patterns. For card 1 on page 45, paper with red tulips and green and yellow envelopes have been used.
6 Cut 2cm (¾in) wide strips from the paper and make separate piles of colour A, colour B and colour C.
7 Fold the edge (approximately 0.7cm (¼in) wide) of each strip over with the patterned or coloured side facing outwards.

Iris folding

8 Take a folded strip of colour A and place it upside down over section 1, exactly against the line of the pattern with the folded edge facing towards the middle. Allow 0.5cm (¼in) to stick out on the left- and right-hand sides and cut the rest off. By doing so, the strip will also stick out slightly over the edge of the pattern at the bottom, so that section 1 is totally covered.

9 Stick the strip to the card on the left- and right-hand sides using a small piece of adhesive tape, but remain 0.5cm (¼in) from the edge of the card.
10 Take a strip of colour B and place it on section 2 of the pattern. Tape the left- and right-hand sides to the card.
11 Take a strip of colour C. Place this on section 3 and stick it into place.
12 Start again with colour A on section 4, colour B on section 5 and colour C on section 6. The strips on sections 1, 4, 7, 10 and 13 of this pattern are all of colour A. The strips of sections 2, 5, 8, 11 and 14 are all of colour B. The strips of sections 3, 6, 9, 12 and 15 are all of colour C.

Finishing

Carefully remove the card after finishing section 15 and stick a piece of holographic paper in the middle on the back of the card. Stick small pieces of double-sided adhesive tape along the edges or use foam tape to bridge the height difference. Remove the protective layer from the double-sided adhesive tape and stick your design on to a double card. Do not use glue, because all the paper strips place pressure on the card.

Step-by-step

1. You will be amazed by the wonderful papers available.

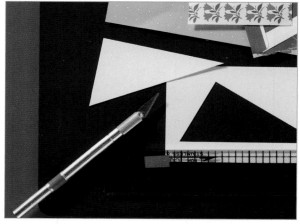

2. Cut the triangular pattern out of the back of a piece of card.

3. Stick the folded strips on to the card.

4. Fold the card open from time to time to check that the design is developing nicely.

Materials

To make the cards:

- ❐ card, for example Canson Mi-Teintes (C), cArt-us (cA) and Papicolor (P)
- ❐ cutting knife, cutting mat
- ❐ ruler with a metal cutting edge (e.g. Securit)
- ❐ adhesive tape
- ❐ double-sided adhesive tape
- ❐ 3D foam tape
- ❐ masking tape
- ❐ corner punches and punches (e.g. MakeMe!, Fiskars, Reuser, Carl and Lim)
- ❐ border ornament punches (e.g. Fiskars, Vaessen)
- ❐ scissors and silhouette scissors
- ❐ figure scissors (e.g. Fiskars)
- ❐ corner scissors (e.g. Fiskars)
- ❐ black fine-liner pen
- ❐ photo glue
- ❐ light box

Iris folding

For the strips:

- ❐ used envelopes
- ❐ iris folding paper (IF paper)
- ❐ origami paper, e.g. Ori-Expres (O–E)
- ❐ pattern paper, 50 × 70cm (19¾ × 27½in) or 70 × 100cm (27½ × 39¼in), e.g. Damen (D).

For the middle of the card:

- ❐ holographic paper

The patterns

Full-size examples of all the patterns are given in this book. Use a light box to copy the outlines on to the card. The shapes are easy to cut out. Specially punched cards are available for the crown, the pram, the good luck hand and the coffee grinder.

Basic triangular pattern

All the cards are made according to the instructions on pages 40–42.

Card 1

- Card: 14.8 × 21cm (5¾ × 8¼in) bright yellow P01, 13 × 7.7cm (5 × 3in) mother-of-pearl red and 12.5 × 7.3cm (5 × 2¾in) natural cA211
- Pattern 1
- 2cm (¾in) wide strips of red tulips pattern paper and green and yellow envelopes
- Holographic paper (gold)
- 3-in-1 corner punch (flowers)

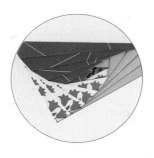

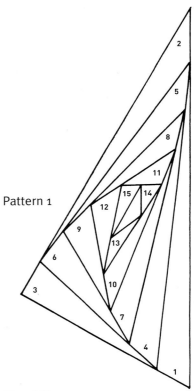

Pattern 1

Card 2

- Card: 14.8 × 21cm (5¾ × 8¼in) purple P46, 13 × 8.7cm (5 × 3½in) orange P135 and 12.5 × 8.2cm (5 × 3¼in) white
- Pattern 1
- 2cm (¾in) wide strips of orange, green flower and purple fan origami paper
- Holographic paper (gold)
- Art Deco corner scissors

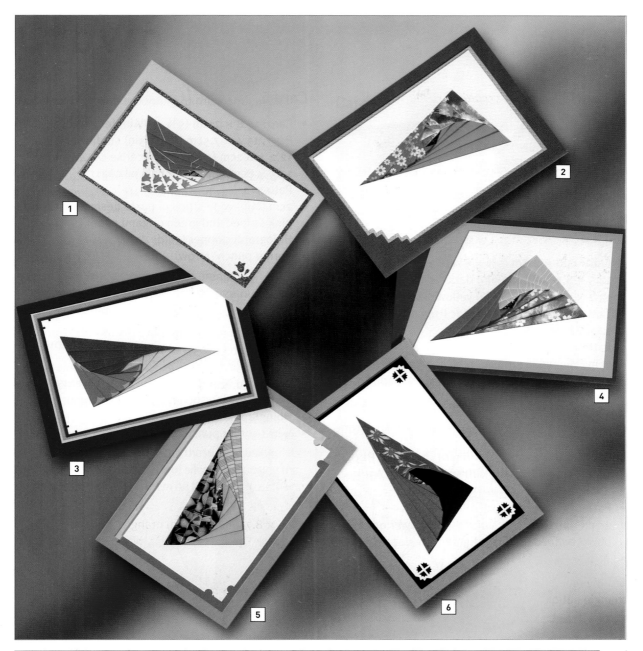

Card 3

- Card: 14.8 × 21cm (5¾ × 8¼in) and 12 × 8.3cm (4¾ × 3¼in) white
- Gold paper, 12.4 × 8.8cm (5 × 3½in)
- Gold embroidered paper, 14.5 × 10cm (5¾ × 4in)
- Pattern 2
- 2cm (¾in) wide strips of gold leaf, pink leaf and pink origami paper and gold paper
- Holographic paper (gold)
- Punch (star)

Card 4

- Card: 14.8 × 21cm (5¾ × 8¼in) brick red C505, 13 × 9cm (5 × 3½in) dark blue P06 and 12 × 8.3cm (4¾ × 3¼in) white
- Pattern 2
- 2cm (¾in) wide strips of sports paper (twice) and blue and brown origami paper
- Holographic paper (silver)
- Corner punch (fountain)

Card 5

- Card: 14.8 × 21cm (5¾ × 8¼in) and 11 × 8cm (4¼ × 3¼in) white, 12.2 × 8.7cm (4¾ × 3½in) rust P186 and 14.3 × 10cm (5¾ × 4in) silver embroidered paper
- Pattern 2
- 2cm (¾in) wide strips of china blue paper, orange origami paper and mat silver holographic paper (×2)
- Holographic paper (silver)
- Punch (crowns)

Card on page 38

- Card: 13 × 26cm (5 × 10¼in) and 9 × 9cm (3½ × 3½in) white and 9.5 × 9.5cm (3¾ × 3¾in) orange cA545
- Grape hyacinths vellum, 12.5 × 12.5cm (5 × 5in)
- Pattern 2
- 2cm (¾in) wide strips of blue leaf vine patterned paper and three blue envelopes
- Holographic paper (orange)
- Punch (hearts)

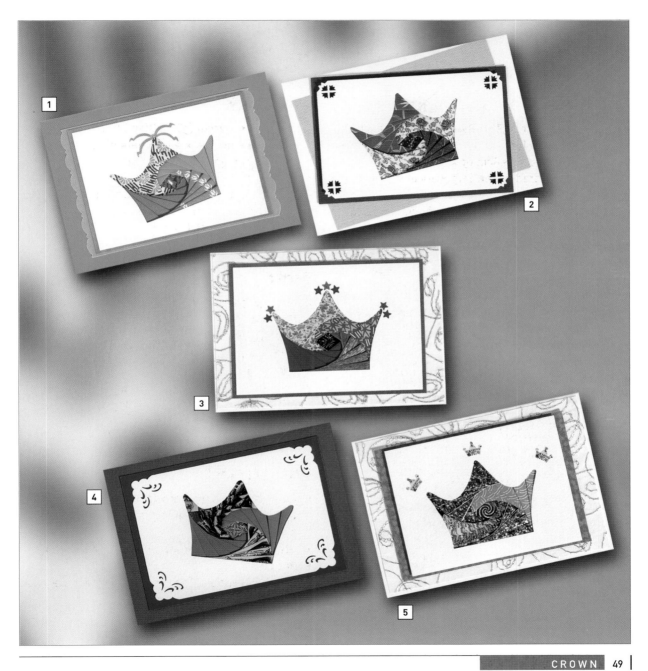

Pram and doll's pram

The pram is made according to the instructions given for card 1 and the doll's pram is made according to the instructions given for card 2.

Card on page 39

- Card: 14.8 × 21cm (5¾ × 8¼in) lilac P14, 14 × 9.5cm (5½ × 3¾in) pale yellow P132, 9.2 × 7.6cm (3½ × 3in) sunflower P134 and 8.5 × 7.3cm (3¼ × 2¾in) pink cA481
- Pink/yellow origami paper, 10.7 × 8.2cm (4¼ × 3¼in)
- Pattern 4
- 2cm (¾in) wide strips of yellow dot, pink flower and pink/yellow origami paper (×2)
- Holographic paper (pink)
- Black fine-liner pen
- Punch (dragonfly)
- 3-in-1 corner punch (celestial)

Card 1

- Card: 14.8 × 21cm (5¾ × 8¼in) cerise P33 and 13.3 × 9.5cm (5¼ × 3¾in) blossom P34
- Pattern 3
- 2cm (¾in) wide strips from a red-pink envelope, purple IF paper, pink flower origami paper and striped origami paper
- Red-pink paper, 9 × 9cm (3½ × 3½in)
- Holographic paper (silver)
- Pink stickers

Cut the basket and the hood out of the light-coloured card and fill them with strips. Copy the frame on to the red-pink paper and cut it out. Draw a circle 2cm (¾in) diameter on a piece of purple paper, fold it double and cut out two wheels. Do the same on a piece of flowered paper using a circle with a diameter of 1.4cm (½in). Stick the frame and the wheels on the card in turn and use stickers to decorate the card.

Card 2

- Card: 14.8 × 21cm (5¾ × 8¼in) golden yellow cA247, 13.3 × 8.4cm (5¼ × 3¼in) pale yellow P132, 12 × 7.5cm (4¾ × 3in) gold P102 and 11.5 × 7.5cm (4½ × 3in) yellow cA275
- Pattern 4
- 2cm (¾in) wide strips from a yellow envelope, beige branch origami paper, beige hearts origami paper and yellow origami paper
- 5 × 3cm (2 × 1¼in) gold leaf origami paper for the hood
- Holographic paper (gold)
- Black fine-liner pen
- Border punch (rose)

Punch the sides of the smallest card and cut out the basket and the hood. Cover the hood using a piece of paper that has been folded double. Draw a circle 1cm (½in) in diameter on a piece of gold leaf paper, fold it double and cut out two wheels. Cut a strip 2.2 × 0.2cm (¾ × ⅛in) for the push bar. Stick everything on the card and draw the black lines.

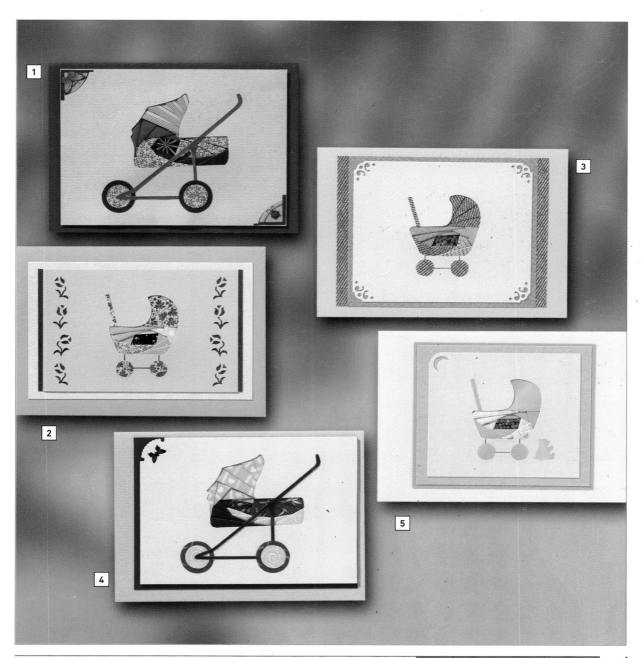

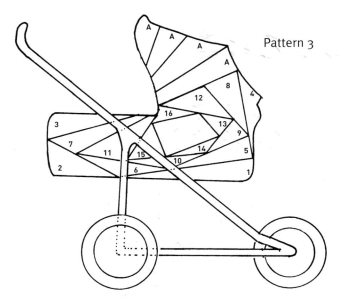

Pattern 3

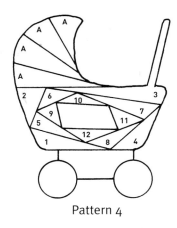

Pattern 4

Card 3

- Card: 14.8 × 21cm (5¾ × 8¼in) yellow cA275 and 10.5 × 8.5cm (4¼ × 3¼in) lemon C101
- Yellow denim paper, 12.5 × 9.2cm (5 × 3½in) and yellow origami paper, 11.2 × 9.2cm (4½ × 3½in)
- Pattern 4
- 2cm (¾in) wide strips of yellow denim and yellow, warm yellow and yellow striped origami paper
- Holographic paper (gold)
- Black fine-liner pen
- 3-in-1 corner punch (lace)

Card 4

- Card: 14.8 × 21cm (5¾ × 8¼in) blossom P34, 13.2 × 9.4cm (5¼ × 3¾in) cherry red P133 and 12.8 × 9cm (5 × 3½) pale pink cA480
- Pattern 3

- 2cm (¾in) wide strips from aubergine and pink envelopes, pink heart origami paper and red-pink flower paper
- Aubergine paper, 9 × 9cm (3½ × 3½in)
- Holographic paper (silver)
- Corner punch (butterfly)

Card 5

- Card: 14.8 × 21cm (5¾ × 8¼in) lemon C101, 10.8 × 8.9cm (4¼ × 3½in) salmon cA482, 10.3 × 8.5cm (4 × 3¼in) sunflower P134 and 9 × 7.5cm (3½ × 3in) yellow
- Pattern 4
- 2cm (¾in) wide strips of yellow flower and striped salmon-yellow origami paper
- Salmon-yellow paper for the hood, 5 × 3cm (2 × 1¼in)
- Holographic paper (gold)
- Black fine-liner pen
- 3-in-1 corner punch (celestial)

Tennis racket and VW Beetle

The tennis racket is made according to the
instructions given for card 1 and the car is made
according to the instructions given for card 2
(pattern on page 54).

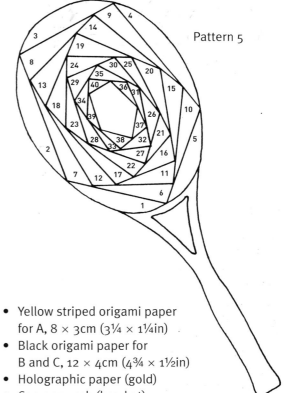

Pattern 5

Card 1

- Card: 14.8 × 21cm (5¾ × 8¼in) aqua blue cA427
  and 13.8 × 9.5cm (5½ × 3¾in) white
- Pattern 5
- 2cm (¾in) wide strips from three blue envelopes
  and two pieces of blue IF paper
- Blue paper for the handle, 7 × 3cm (2¾ × 1¼in)
- Holographic paper (silver)
- Multi corner punch

Punch two corners of the white card and cut out
the racket without the handle. Fill the oval with the
strips of paper. Use a pencil to copy the handle on to
the blue paper. Cut it out and stick it on the card.

Card 2

- Card: 14.8 × 21cm (5¾ × 8¼in) wine red P36 and
  14.5 × 9cm (5¾ × 3½in) sand yellow C407
- Pattern 6
- 2cm (¾in) wide strips from beige and red
  envelopes, yellow origami paper (×2), black
  origami paper and angel paper

- Yellow striped origami paper
  for A, 8 × 3cm (3¼ × 1¼in)
- Black origami paper for
  B and C, 12 × 4cm (4¾ × 1½in)
- Holographic paper (gold)
- Corner punch (bracket)
- Black fine-liner pen

Cut the car out of the back of the sand yellow card
and cut along the dotted line at the bottom. Place the
card upside down on the pattern. Cover the A sections
with striped paper and the B and C sections with black
paper. Fill the car with the iris folding strips. Turn the
card over. Draw two wheels of 2cm (¾in) diameter, cut
them out and stick them on the card. Draw the aerial.

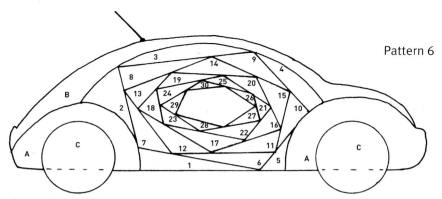

Card 3

- Card: 14.8 × 21cm (5¾ × 8¼in) sweetcorn C470 and 14.4 × 9.5cm (5¾ × 3¾in) azure C590
- Pattern 5
- 2cm (¾in) wide strips from one beige envelope and two red envelopes and plaited red paper
- Beige paper for the handle, 7 × 3cm (2¾ × 1¼in)
- Red paper for the second racket, 13 × 5cm (5 × 2in)
- Holographic paper (gold)
- 3-in-1 corner punch (lace)

After finishing the iris folding, cut out the red tennis racket and the beige handle and stick them on the card.

Card 4

- Card: 14.8 × 21cm (5¾ × 8¼in) old red cA517, 13.7 × 8cm (5½ × 3¼in) beige and two pieces of 13.7 × 3cm (5½ × 1¼in) off-white
- Pattern 6
- 2cm (¾in) wide strips from two red envelopes and three red origami papers
- Red beige striped origami paper for section A, 8 × 3cm (3¼ × 1¼in)
- Red envelope for sections B and C, 12 × 4cm (4¾ × 1½in)
- Holographic paper (bronze)
- Border punch (rope)
- Black fine-liner pen

Punch the small strips of card and stick them at the top and bottom of the beige card.

Card 5

- Card: 14.8 × 21cm (5¾ × 8¼in) and 13.8 × 9.5cm (5½ × 3¾in) white and 14.2 × 9.9cm (5¼ × 4in) dark blue P06
- Pattern 5
- 2cm (¾in) wide strips from four blue envelopes and one red envelope
- Cup from sports paper
- Blue paper for the handle, 7 × 3cm (2¾ × 1¼in)
- Holographic paper (silver)
- Corner scissors (nostalgia)

Card 6

- Card: 14.8 × 21cm (5¾ × 8¼in) blue and 14 × 8.8cm (5½ × 3½in) cream
- Dark blue envelope, 14 × 9.3cm (5½ × 3¾in)
- Pattern 6
- 2cm (¾in) wide strips from three blue envelopes, marbled paper and marbled origami paper
- Marbled origami paper for section A, 8 × 3cm (3¼ × 1¼in)
- Dark blue paper for sections B and C, 12 × 4cm (4¾ × 1½in)
- Holographic paper (silver)
- Black fine-liner pen
- Corner punch (spear)

Good luck hand

All the cards are made according to the instructions given for card 1.

Card 1

- Card: 14.8 × 21cm (5¾ × 8¼in) dark green cA309, 14 × 9.4cm (5½ × 3¾in) spring green cA305 and 13.5 × 9cm (5¼ × 3½in) white
- Pattern 7
- 2.5cm (1in) wide strips of green cloverleaf, striped and green origami paper and green paper chain pattern paper
- Holographic paper (gold)
- Corner scissors (celestial)

Punch two corners of the white card and cut out the hand. Cut the paper strip for section 25 in the correct shape.

Card 2

- Card: 14.8 × 21cm (5¾ × 8¼in) golden yellow cA247, 13.5 × 9.7cm (5¼ × 3¾in) terracotta cA549, 13 × 9.2cm (5 × 3½in) orange P135 and 12.5 × 8.7cm (5 × 3½in) white
- Pattern 7
- 2.5cm (1in) wide strips of gold IF paper (yellow set), a yellow envelope, salmon origami paper and tulip pattern paper
- Holographic paper (gold)
- Corner scissors (regal)
- 4-in-1 embossing punch

Carefully punch the corners of the white card using the embossing punch and cut the corners of the orange card using the corner scissors.

Card 3

- Card: 14.8 × 21cm (5¾ × 8¼in) brick red C505 and 14.8 × 9.3cm (5¾ × 3¾in) white
- Transparent candy pink paper P150, 14.5 × 9.7cm (5¾ × 3¾in)
- Pattern 7
- 2.5cm (1in) wide strips of wine red, pink, pink dot and old rose origami paper
- Holographic paper (silver)
- Circle cutter and Victorian punch

Cut the curve at the top of the white card and punch two small patterns. Cut the hand out and fill it with strips. Also cut a curve at the top of the transparent paper.

Card 4

- Card: 14.8 × 21cm (5¾ × 8¼in) royal blue P136 and 13 × 9cm white (5 × 3½in)
- Pattern 7
- 2.5cm (1in) wide strips from two blue envelopes and two pieces of blue IF paper
- Holographic paper (silver)
- 3-in-1 corner punch (heart)

Punch one corner of the white card and decorate the card with hearts.

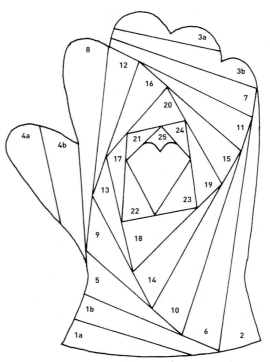

Pattern 7

Kaleidoscope cards

Both cards are made according to the instructions given for card 1 and fit in an A4 envelope.

Card 1

- Card: 20 × 29cm (7¾ × 11½in) orange C453, 25.3 × 19.2cm (10 × 7½in) sand yellow C407 and 22 × 18.2cm (8¾ × 7¼in) Christmas red P43
- Pattern 8
- 2cm (¾in) wide strips of red, orange and yellow mother-of-pearl origami paper
- Holographic paper (gold)
- Self-adhesive corners

Cut the hexagon out of the red card. Fold three orange and three yellow strips, 8 × 1.5cm (3¼ × ½in) into strips of 8 × 0.6cm (3¼ × ¼in) to start the pattern. Place them on the starting sections of the pattern in alternating colours. Stick one end to the card, cut them at an angle or weave them and stick them all down together. Two sections of each triangle will now be covered. Continue as described in the techniques section (page 41). Decorate the card with four corners.

Card 2

- Card: 20 × 29cm (7¾ × 11½in) green cA367, 19 × 26.3cm (7½ × 10¼in) dark blue cA417 and 18 × 19.6cm (7 × 7¾in) cream cA241
- Sea green mother-of-pearl card, 6 × 18cm (2¼ × 7in)
- Pattern 8
- 2cm (¾in) wide strips of blue rose and blue lion paper and dark blue origami paper
- Holographic paper (sea green)
- Punch

If you wish, use a coloured pencil to colour in the copy of this pattern before doing the iris folding. Note: the colours change position. Punch the edges of the blue card. Make six strips as described above, but this time make two dark blue strips, two blue strips with lions and two blue strips with roses. Place them on the starting sections in alternating colours. Continue as described for card 1. Cut two strips 3 × 18cm (1¼ × 7in) from the mother-of-pearl paper and stick them at the top and bottom of the cream card.

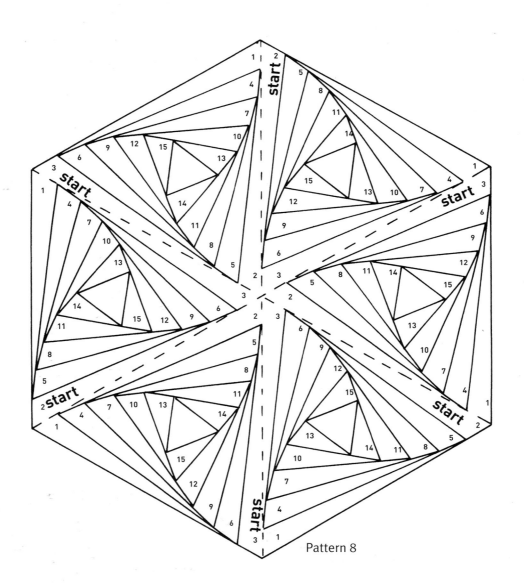

Pattern 8

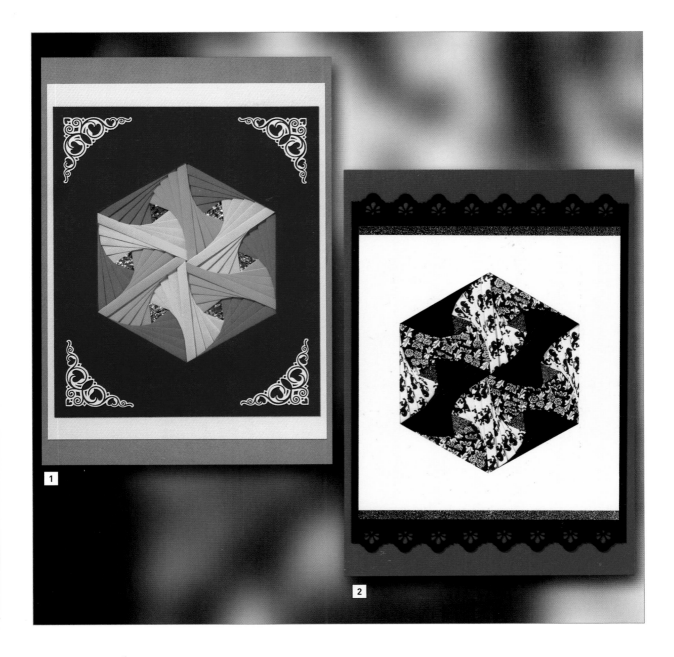

1

2

Coffee grinder

The coffee grinder is made according to the instructions given for card 1.

Card on page 40

- Card: 13 × 26cm (5 × 10¼in) cerise P33, 11.4 × 11cm (4½ × 4¼in) blossom P34 and 11.4 × 9.8cm (4½ × 3¾in) white
- Pattern 9
- 2cm (¾in) wide strips of classic patterned paper (×2) and red-pink and pink origami paper
- Strip of classic patterned paper, 18 × 2cm (7 × ¾in) for sections A, C and D
- Red-pink paper, 5 × 4cm (2 × 1½in) for section B
- Holographic paper (gold)
- 3-in-1 corner punch (lace)

Card 1

- Card: 14.8 × 21cm (5¾ × 8¼in) dark yellow cA245, 13 × 9.4cm (5 × 3¾in) terracotta cA549 and 12.5 × 8.8cm (5 × 3½in) white
- Pattern 9
- 2cm (¾in) wide strips from yellow, orange and brown IF paper
- Blue envelope, 7 × 5cm (2¾ × 2in) for sections A, C and D
- Brown envelope, 5 × 4cm (2 × 1½in) for section B
- Holographic paper (gold)
- 3-in-1 punch (lace)

Punch two corners of the white card and cut out section B and the coffee pot. Cover section B with brown paper. Fill the coffee pot with the strips of IF paper. Turn the card over. Copy sections A, C and D on to blue paper. Cut them out and stick them on the card. Stick the handle between sections A and B. Copy section C onto blue paper. Cut it out and stick it on the bar under section B.

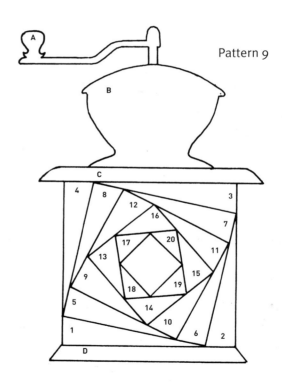

Pattern 9

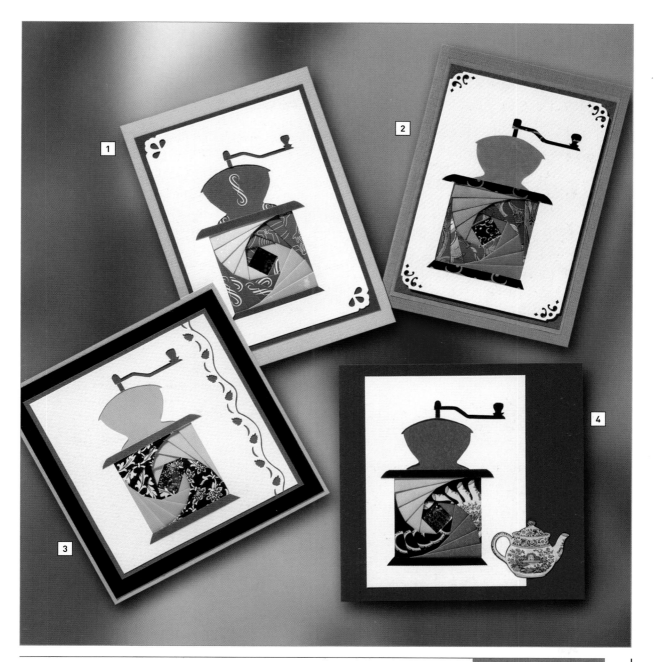

Card 2

- Card: 14.8 × 21cm (5¾ × 8¼in) violet P20, 13 × 9cm (5 × 3½in) lavender blue C150 and 12.3 × 8.7cm (4¾ × 3½in) white
- Orange origami paper, 13.5 × 9.4cm (5¼ × 3¾in)
- Pattern 9
- 2cm (¾in) wide strips of orange and old rose origami paper and orange and old rose classic patterned paper
- Strip of dark classic patterned paper for sections A, C and D
- Old rose paper, 5 × 4cm (2 × 1½in) for section B
- Holographic paper (gold)
- 3-in-1 corner punch (lace)

Card 3

- Card: 13 × 26cm (5 × 10¼in) raw sienna C374, 12.5 × 12.5cm (5 × 5in) marine blue cA420, 11 × 11cm (4¼ × 4¼in) red earth C130 and 10.5 × 10.5cm (4¼ × 4¼in) off-white
- Pattern 9
- 2cm (¾in) wide strips of diagonal blue paper (×2), a beige envelope and pink origami paper
- Brown paper, 7 × 5cm (2¾ × 2in) for sections A, C and D
- Pink origami paper, 5 × 4cm (2 × 1½in) for section B
- Holographic paper (silver)
- Border punch (leaves)

Punch the edge of the smallest card.

Card 4

- Card: 13 × 26cm (5 × 10¼in) aqua blue cA427 and 11.5 × 8.5cm (4½ × 3¼in) white
- Pattern 9
- 2cm (¾in) wide strips of blue teapot patterned paper, a blue envelope and blue IF paper
- Dark blue patterned paper, 7 × 5cm (2¾ × 2in) for sections A, C and D
- Blue IF paper, 5 × 4cm (2 × 1½in) for section B
- Holographic paper (silver)
- Teapot from the patterned paper

Magician's hat

The magician's hat is made according to the instructions given for card 1.

Card 1

- Card: 13 × 26cm (5 × 10¼in) aqua, 11.5 × 11.5cm (4½ × 4½in) white and 11 × 11cm (4¼ × 4¼in) marine blue cA420
- Pattern 10
- 2cm (¾in) wide strips from aqua and blue-white envelopes
- Holographic paper (snowflake)
- Holographic paper (silver)
- 3-in-1 corner punch (celestial)

Punch the upper corners of the blue card and cut the hat out of the blue card without the brim. To give it some extra strength, stick double-sided adhesive tape on the card marked by the cross, before attaching the marine blue card to the white card. Fill the hat with strips. Copy brim A and stick it on the front.

Card 2

- Card: 13 × 26cm (5 × 10¼in) royal blue P136 and 9.5 × 9.5cm (3¾ × 3¾in) white
- Pattern 10
- 2cm (¾in) wide strips from aqua and blue envelopes and blue flower origami paper
- Holographic paper (silver)
- Corner punch (arrow)

Create a sense of speed using strips of holographic paper, 4 × 0.15cm (1½ × ⅛in).

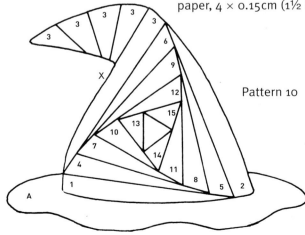

Pattern 10

Card 3

- Card: 13 × 26cm (5 × 10¼in) cerise cA440, 11 × 11cm (4¼ × 4¼in) purple mirror P124 and 10 × 10cm (4 × 4in) purple cA426
- Pattern 10
- 2cm (¾in) wide strips of pink, pale pink and lilac flower origami paper
- Corner punch (party design)

Leave 0.1cm (⅛in) of space between the hat and the brim.

Card 4

- Card: 13 × 26cm (5 × 10¼in) pale yellow P132, 11 × 11cm (4¼ × 4¼in) metallic brown and 10.5 × 10.5cm (4¼ × 4¼in) dark yellow cA245
- Pattern 10
- 2cm (¾in) wide strips of brown and brown branch origami paper and Angel pattern paper
- Holographic paper (gold)
- 3-in-1 corner punch (celestial)
- Punch (rabbit)

Card 5

- Card: 13 × 26cm (5 × 10¼in) grey, 11 × 11cm (4¼ × 4¼in) purple cA426 and 10.7 × 10.7cm (4¼ × 4¼in) orange cA545
- Pattern 10
- 2cm (¾in) wide strips of purple and grey envelopes and peacock tail origami paper
- Corner punch (fountain)

Decorate the hat using a cut-out peacock's tail.

Card 6

- Card: 13 × 26cm (5 × 10¼in) green cA367, 10.5 × 10.5cm (4¼ × 4¼in) spring green cA305 and 10 × 10cm (4 × 4in) white
- Pattern 10
- 2cm (¾in) wide strips from green and light green envelopes and green flower origami paper
- Holographic paper (gold)
- 3-in-1 corner punch (celestial)

Cut the brim of the hat out of green and light green paper. Stick them under the hat slightly offset.

Card 7

- Card: 13 × 26cm (5 × 10¼in) black, 11 × 11cm (4¼ × 4¼in) brick red P35, 10.5 × 10.5cm (4¼ × 4¼in) white and 10 × 10cm (4 × 4in) dark blue P06
- Pattern 10
- 2cm (¾in) wide strips of dog pattern paper, bronze origami paper and a light blue envelope
- Holographic paper (silver)
- Corner punch (bracket)

Thread a strip of bronze paper, 1.5cm (½in) wide, through the punch and punch every 0.2cm (⅛in) to make the bats.

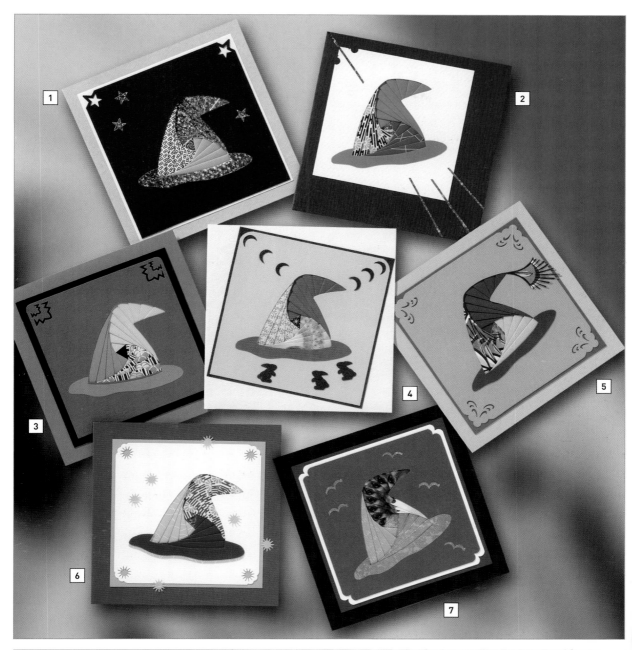

Chapter 3: Iris Folding: a Full Year

Techniques

The starting point for iris folding is the pattern. Trace the outline of the pattern on the back of your card and cut it out. Fill the opening with strips of folded paper, working from the outside in. As you are working at the back of the card, you are, in fact, working with a mirror image. Once you have finished the iris folding, attach the decorated card to another card. For a square pattern, select four different pieces of paper with patterns and colours that combine or contrast nicely.

Cut all the pieces of paper into strips in the same way, for example from left to right. Depending on the pattern, you will need between four and eight strips. The width of the strips also depends on the pattern and is stated in the instructions given for each card. First, you need to give the strips a lengthwise folded edge and then group them according to colour. Next, you cover each section of the pattern in turn by following the numbers (1, 2, 3, 4, 5, etc.), using a different colour each time. Place the strips on the card with the folded edge facing the centre of the pattern, then attach the left- and right-hand sides of the strips to the card using adhesive tape. Finally, use an attractive piece of holographic paper to cover the hole in the middle.

The basic pattern

(see card 1 on pages 74 and 75 and the step-by-step section on page 72)

It is important to start with the basic pattern, as it will teach you the unique folding and sticking techniques needed for all the other patterns. You will quickly get used to the iris folding technique.

1. Place the white card, measuring 13 × 10cm (5 × 4in), with the *back* towards you.
2. With a pencil, trace the outline of the vase on your card using a light table. Cut out the pattern.
3. Using adhesive tape, attach a copy of the base pattern, the vase on page 76, to your cutting mat.
4. Place the opening in your white card exactly over the pattern (with the back of the white card facing you) and, using masking tape, attach the card to your cutting mat, but *only* on the left-hand side.
5. Choose four pieces of paper in different patterns. For card 1 on page 75, the following papers were used: origami paper with a bright pink design, old rose, pink and white and plain pink.
6. Cut strips 2cm (¾in) wide and divide them into colour A, colour B, colour C and colour D.
7. Fold each strip lengthwise, creating an edge – about 0.7cm (¼in). The patterned or coloured side of the paper needs to be folded outwards.

Iris folding

8. Take a strip of colour A and place it, patterned side down, on section A at the bottom, neatly against the line indicated on the pattern. Make sure the folded edge of the strip is pointing towards the middle. Leave 0.5cm (¼in) of the strip extending on both the left and right side and cut off the excess. The strip should also extend a little at the bottom of the pattern, so that section A is completely covered. Using a little bit of adhesive tape, attach the strip on the left- and right-hand side to the card, making sure you keep clear of the card edge by about 0.5cm (¼in).
9. Repeat the same process for the upper sections A.
10. Using colour A again, put a new strip on section 1 of the pattern. Tape the left- and right-hand sides.
11. Attach colour B to section 2.
12. Attach colour C to section 3.
13. Attach colour D to section 4.
14. Continue by putting colour A on section 5, colour B on section 6, colour C on section 7 and colour D on section 8.

In this pattern, the strips on sections 1, 5, 9, 13 and 17 are all of colour A. The strips on 2, 6, 10, 14 and 18 are all of colour B, the strips on 3, 7, 11, 15 and 19 are of colour C and the strips on 4, 8, 12, 16 and 20 are all of colour D.

Finishing

Detach the card after you have covered section 20. Cover the centre with a piece of holographic paper (again, on the back). To finish the card, you can use punches, scissors and cut-out paper embellishments. Attach double-sided tape to the edges of the card, or use 3D foam tape to allow for the thickness of the strips attached. Remove the protective layer and attach your piece to a single and/or double card in a contrasting colour. Do not use glue, as the strips of paper put pressure on the decorated card.

Step-by-step

1. Collect beautiful papers from all over the world!

2. Cut the vase from the back of single card.

3. Following the numbers, attach both the pattern and the card to your cutting mat and stick on the folded strips.

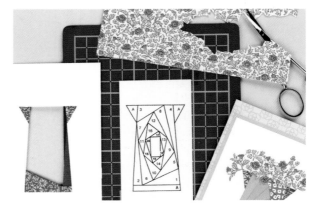

4. Open out the card from time to time to check that the pattern is developing nicely. Decorate the front of the card with cut-out flowers.

Materials

To make the cards:

- ☐ card, for example Papicolor (P)
- ☐ cutting knife, cutting mat
- ☐ ruler with a metal cutting edge (e.g. Securit)
- ☐ adhesive tape
- ☐ double-sided adhesive tape
- ☐ 3D foam tape
- ☐ masking tape
- ☐ corner punches and punches (e.g. Fiskars)
- ☐ scissors and silhouette scissors
- ☐ border stickers
- ☐ circle cutter
- ☐ black fine-liner pen
- ☐ photo glue
- ☐ light box

Iris folding

Strips of paper made of:

- ☐ used envelopes
- ☐ wrapping paper
- ☐ origami paper
- ☐ floral paper
- ☐ magazine pages

For the centre:

- ☐ holographic paper
- ☐ wrapping paper

The patterns

The patterns for all the cards in this book are full size. Copy the outlines using a light box. In general, the shapes are easily cut or clipped out of the card.

Basic pattern: vase

All cards are made following the instructions given for the basic pattern (see pages 70 to 72).

Card 1

- Card: 14.8 × 21cm (5¾ × 8¼in) pink fantasia P769, 13 × 10cm (5 × 4in) light blue P61 and 12 × 9cm (4¾ × 3½in) white
- Vase pattern
- 2cm (¾in) wide strips of paper in the following colours: bright pink pattern, old rose, pink and white, and plain pink
- 9 × 5cm (3½ × 2in) paper with flowers in blue and pink

After completing the iris folding, fill the vase with a bouquet of partially cut-out flowers, which you can attach to the card using photo glue.

Card 2

- Card: 14.8 × 21cm (5¾ × 8¼in) light yellow and 14.8 × 8.2cm (5¾ × 3¼in) white
- Vase pattern
- 2cm (¾in) wide strips of paper in the following colours: gold, pink/yellow, plain yellow, and yellow with white flowers
- 4 × 8cm (1½ × 3¼in) green paper for the leaves
- Holographic paper (gold)

Attach a copy of the leaf design to the green paper, cut it out and, using tape, attach it above the vase. Cut out three tulips from the pink/yellow paper and attach them to the stems. Attach strips of 14.8 × 1cm (5¾ × ½in) gold paper left and right behind the white card.

Card 3

- Card: 15 × 30cm (6 × 11¾in) yellow P610 and 13 × 13cm (5 × 5in) white
- Vase pattern
- 2cm (¾in) wide strips of paper in the following colours: dark blue, blue design and blue
- Paper: various shades of yellow and blue paper for the flowers; various shades of green for the leaf
- Holographic paper (blue)
- Punches (large and medium flower) and matching relief punches
- Punch (fern leaf)

After the iris folding, attach the double-sided tape along the sides at the back of the white card. Using the punches, make nine blue and seven yellow big and small flowers and then give them shape by using the relief punch. Make ten green leaves. Assemble the bouquet and attach it with photo glue.

Card 4

- Card: 14.8 × 21cm (5¾ × 8¼in) lavender P21 and 14.8 × 8cm (5¾ × 3¼in) white
- Vase pattern
- 2cm (¾in) wide strips of paper in the following colours: apple green, light green pattern and blue flower pattern
- Floral wrapping paper

Cut three flowers out of wrapping paper and, using glue, attach them above the vase. Attach small strips in the light green design on the left and the right behind the white card.

Card 5

- Card: 14.8 × 21cm (5¾ × 8¼in) almond green and 13.5 × 9cm (5¼ × 3½in) white
- Vase pattern
- 2cm (¾in) wide strips of paper in the following colours: dark green, green leaf design, light green and a green and white striped pattern
- Various shades of pink paper for the flowers
- 10 × 4cm (4 × 1½in) green striped paper for the leaves
- Punches: medium flower and matching relief punch; fern leaf punch

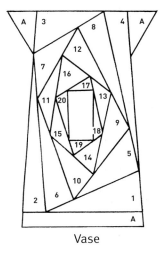

Vase

After the iris folding, attach the double-sided tape along the sides at the back of the white card. Punch nine pink flowers, which you then divide into four double and one single flower. Cut very thin strips of pink paper. Scrunch them up into little balls and, using glue, attach them at the centre of each of the five flowers. After the glue has dried, cut the centres open with the tip of your scissors to loosen them slightly. Punch the leaves, add a little glue and attach them above and behind the flowers.

Phone and camera

The mobile phone is made using the instructions for card 1, the ultra-compact camera using the instructions for card 3.

Card 1

- Card: 14.8 × 21cm (5¾ × 8¼in) mint green, 12 × 8cm (4¾ × 3¼in) white and 11.5 × 7.5cm (4¼ × 3in) cornflower blue
- Blue paper, 14.8 × 8cm (5¾ × 3¼in)
- Mobile phone pattern
- 1.5cm (½in) wide strips of paper in blue, green, mint green striped and white
- Black paper, 9 × 5cm (3½ × 2in) for the mobile phone and green paper, 5 × 5cm (2 × 2in) for the buttons
- Border sticker (blue)

Cut the numbered part of the pattern only out of the back of the cornflower blue card. After the iris folding, cut out the mobile phone from the black paper, cut out the screen and attach it to the front of the cornflower blue card.

Draw the buttons on green paper, cut them out and attach them. Attach the border sticker to the mobile phone. Attach the cornflower blue card to the white card. Attach the blue paper to the front right-hand side of the double mint green card. Attach the white card to the double card at an angle.

Card 2

- Card: 14.8 × 21cm (5¾ × 8¼in) bright pink and 11 × 7cm (4¼ × 2¾in) white
- Pink paper, 12 × 8cm (4¾ × 3¼in)
- Mobile phone pattern
- 1.5cm (½in) wide strips of paper in white/pink pattern, pinkish red, salmon pink and pink
- Bright pink metallic origami paper, 9 × 5cm (3½ × 2in)
- Salmon pink origami paper with hearts, 5 × 5cm (2 × 2in)
- Holographic paper (pink)
- Punch (hearts)

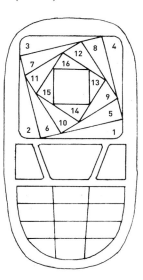

Mobile phone

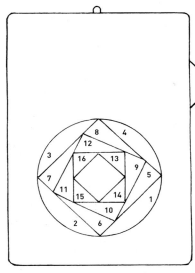

Camera

Card 3

- Card: 7.5 × 21cm (3 × 8¼in) pink and 9 × 6.5cm (3½ × 2½in) black
- Paper: 9 × 6.5cm (3½ × 2½in) silver design and a circle of mat silver, diameter 0.5cm (¼in)
- Camera pattern
- 1.5cm (½in) wide strips of paper in dark blue, purple blue check, plain blue and blue stripes
- Holographic paper (silver)
- 12cm (4¾in) thin black cord
- Circle cutter

Cut a circle of diameter 4cm (1½in) out of the black card, following the pattern. After the iris folding, attach the cut-out silver camera to the front. Cut a mat silver ring of width 0.5cm (¼in) and place it around the coloured strips.

Card 4

- Card: 7.5 × 21cm (3 × 8¼in) silver, 9.2 × 6.7cm (3½ × 2¾in) grey and 9 × 6.5cm (3½ × 2½in) black
- Camera pattern
- 1.5cm (½in) wide strips of paper in yellow green, blue green, apple green and blue pattern
- Holographic paper (silver)
- Various silver stickers

After the iris folding, decorate the circle with a border of stickers. Also make an eyelet and cord.

Card 5

- Card: 7.5 × 21cm (3 × 8¼in) pale blue and 9 × 6.5cm (3½ × 2½in) black
- Paper: 9 × 6.5cm (3½ × 2½in) mat silver and a circle of black, diameter 0.5cm (¼in)
- Camera pattern
- 1.5cm (½in) wide strips of paper in blue and white designs
- Holographic paper (silver)
- Border stickers (silver)
- 12cm (4¾in) thin black cord

Swan and daffodil

The swan is made following the instructions for card 1, and the daffodil following card 2.

Card 1

- Card: 13 × 26cm (5 × 10¼in) pink P15 and 11 × 11cm (4¼ × 4¼in) blue P06
- Swan pattern
- 2cm (¾in) wide strips of paper in white and pink pattern
- White paper, 8 × 4cm (3¼ × 1½in) for head and wave
- Border stickers (lace)

Cut only the body out of the blue card. Make four groups of paper strips, two in white and two with the pink design, and fill in the body. After the iris folding, trace the neck and wave on to white paper. Cut everything out and attach to the front of the card. Draw on the eye and decorate with lace border stickers.

Card 2

- Card: 14.8 × 21cm (5¾ × 8¼in) bright green P13 and 12.5 × 9.5cm (5 × 3¾in) white
- Paper with 'green scratches' design, 12 × 9cm (4¾ × 3½in)
- Daffodil pattern
- 2cm (¾in) wide strips of paper in orange, salmon and yellow
- Holographic paper (bronze)
- Green paper, 9 × 2cm (3½ × ¾in) for stem and leaf
- Yellow paper, 9 × 2cm (3½ × ¾in) for A, B and C

First, glue the 'green scratches' paper to the centre of the white card. Allow to dry. Turn over the card and make a cut-out of the numbered part of the flower only. After the iris folding, cut parts A, B and C out of yellow paper and the stem and leaf out of green paper. Attach everything.

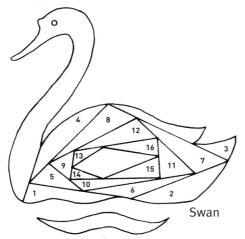

Swan

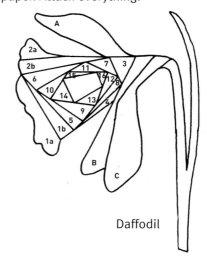

Daffodil

Card 3

- Card: 13 × 26cm (5 × 10¼in) orange P135, 11 × 11cm (4¼ × 4¼in) white and 10.5 × 10.5cm (4¼ × 4¼in) blue P06
- Swan pattern
- 2cm (¾in) wide strips of paper in white and orange design
- White paper, 8 × 4cm (3¼ × 1½in) for head and wave
- Text sticker (yellow)
- 20cm (7¾in) thin white ribbon for the bow

Card 4

- Card: 14.8 × 21cm (5¾ × 8¼in) light green, 13.5 × 9.5cm (5¼ × 3¾in) green design and 11.8 × 9cm (4¾ × 3½in) green
- Daffodil pattern
- 2cm (¾in) wide strips of paper in four different shades of yellow
- Holographic paper (gold)
- Green paper, 9 × 2cm (3½ × ¾in) for stem and leaf
- Butterfly sticker

Card 5

- Card: 13 × 26cm (5 × 10¼in) lilac, 11 × 11cm (4¼ × 4¼in) violet, 10.7 × 10.7cm (4¼ × 4¼in) white and 10 × 10cm (4 × 4in) blue P06
- Swan pattern
- 2cm (¾in) wide strips of paper in white and violet design
- White paper, 8 × 4cm (3¼ × 1½in) for head and wave
- Corner punch (sun)

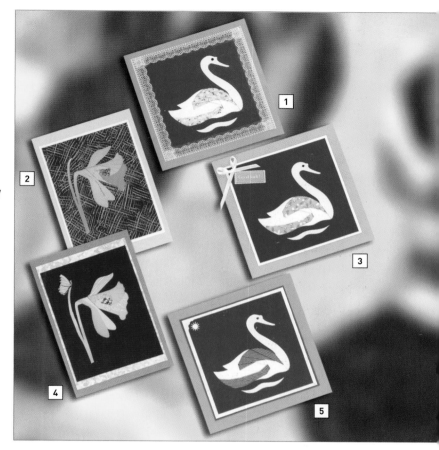

Medal and cup

The medal is made using the instructions for card 1, and the cup using those for card 3.

Card 1

- Card: 14.8 × 21cm (5¾ × 8¼in) orange C453 and 13.5 × 8cm (5¼ × 3¼in) white
- Gold paper, 13.5 × 1cm (5¼ × ½in) (×2)
- Medal pattern
- 2cm (¾in) wide strips of paper in blue, orange, blue pattern and red/yellow
- Orange paper, 4 × 3cm (1½ × 1¼in) and gold paper, 4 × 4cm (1½ × 1½in) for pendant
- Holographic paper (gold)

Cut the medal out of the white paper, omitting the pendant. Fill the pattern with strips. With a pencil, trace the 'metal' parts of the pendant on to gold paper up to the dotted line. Trace the middle strip on to orange paper. Cut everything out. Use photo glue to attach the gold parts, followed by the orange middle part.

Card 2

- Card: 14.8 × 21cm (5¾ × 8¼in) mat gold and 13 × 7.5cm (5 × 3in) white
- Paper: 13 × 1cm (5 × ½in) dark red (×2) and 1 × 7.5cm (½ × 3in) red (×2)
- Medal pattern
- 2cm (¾in) wide strips of paper in pinkish red, burgundy/beige stripes, red and dark red pattern
- Burgundy/beige stripe paper, 4 × 3cm (1½ × 1¼in) and mat gold paper, 4 × 4cm (1½ × 1½in) for pendant
- Holographic paper (bronze)

Card 3

- Card: 14.8 × 21cm (5¾ × 8¼in) blue, 13 × 9cm (5 × 3½in) gold and 11.5 × 8.5cm (4½ × 3¼in) white
- Cup pattern
- 2cm (¾in) wide strips of paper in blue/beige stripe, blue, blue/gold thin stripe and gold
- Holographic paper (gold)
- Self-adhesive gold paper for base and handles
- Border stickers (gold)

Cut the numbered part of the cup out of the back of the white card and fill it with strips. Place a copy of the base and handles on the back of the gold paper, cut out and attach around the cup. Attach the white card to the sheet of gold card and attach the whole to double white card. Decorate with border stickers.

Card 4

- Card: 14.8 × 21cm (5¾ × 8¼in) white and 13.5 × 9cm (5¼ × 3½in) mat blue
- Paper: origami blue fireworks design, 11.5 × 9cm (4½ × 3½in) and red, 1 × 9cm (½ × 3½in) (×2)
- Cup pattern
- 2cm (¾in) wide strips of paper in white (×2) and blue (×2)
- Holographic paper (blue)
- Self-adhesive red paper for base and handles

Attach the fireworks design paper to the blue card first, and let it dry.

Card 5

- Card: 14.8 × 21cm (5¾ × 8¼in) blue and 14.8 × 8.5cm (5¾ × 3¼in) white
- Paper with multi-coloured stripe pattern, 13.5 × 7.5cm (5¼ × 3in) and dark blue, 1 × 13.5cm (½ × 5¼in) (×2)
- Medal pattern
- 2cm (¾in) wide strips of paper in four different gold papers
- Gold paper, 4 × 3cm (1½ × 1¼in) and blue paper, 4 × 4cm (1½ × 1½in) for the pendant
- Holographic paper (blue)
- Border sticker (gold)

First, glue a piece of dark blue paper, 1 × 13.5cm (½ × 5¼in), left and right of the white card. Attach the multi-coloured stripe patterned paper to the white card. Wait until everything is properly dry and then cut the medal from the back.

Card 6

- Card: 14.8 × 21cm (5¾ × 8¼in) red, 12.5 × 9cm (5 × 3½in) blue and 12 × 8.5cm (4¾ × 3¼in) white
- Cup pattern
- 2cm (¾in) wide strips of paper in red, orange and blue (×2)
- Holographic paper (silver)
- Self-adhesive mat blue paper for base and handles

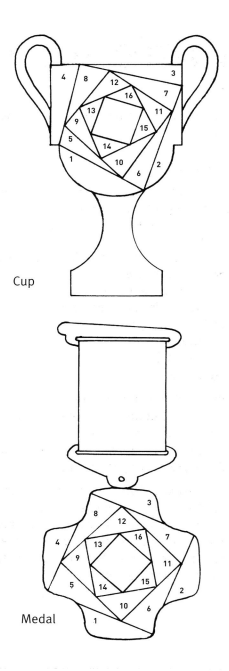

Cup

Medal

Gnome and bucket

Use card 1 to make the gnome and card 4 to make the bucket.

1 Garden gnome

- Card: 14.8 × 21cm (5¾ × 8¼in) Fantasia flower yellow P774, 11.5 × 8.5cm (4½ × 3¼in) yellow P610 and 11 × 8cm (4¼ × 3¼in) white
- Gnome pattern
- 1.5cm (½in) wide strips of paper in red, origami green design and yellow
- Paper: 6 × 4cm (2¼ × 1½in) red, 3 × 3cm (1¼ × 1¼in) soft yellow and 2 × 6cm (¾ × 2¼in) yellow
- Holographic paper (green)
- Sticker edges (red)
- Sticker (butterfly)

Cut the numbered part of the gnome out of the white card, up to the dotted line at the bottom. During the iris folding, pay attention to the following: section 21 is missing, so pass over 1 strip of green design; section 24 has a ready-cut tip!

Trace the hat, beard and arms on to red paper and cut out. Trace the face on to soft yellow paper and cut out. Attach the arms, hat, face and beard. Trace one clog on to yellow paper, fold in two along the dotted line to 2 × 3cm (¾ × 1¼in), cut out, but leave the back intact. Attach the clogs.

2 Forest gnome

- Card: 14.8 × 21cm (5¾ × 8¼in) moss green, 14 × 9cm (5½ × 3½in) Fantasia green P779 and 11 × 7.5cm (4¼ × 3in) white
- Gnome pattern
- 1.5cm (½in) wide strips of paper in green, dark brown design, light green and light brown pattern
- Paper: 6 × 4cm (2¼ × 1½in) green for hat and arms; 3 × 3cm (1¼ × 1¼in) beige for face; and 2 × 6cm (¾ × 2¼in) brown for boots
- Holographic paper (gold)

Gnome

Bucket

3 House gnome

- Card: 14.8 × 21cm (5¾ × 8¼in) violet, 12 × 8.5cm (4¾ × 3¼in) lilac and 11.5 × 8cm (4½ × 3¼in) white
- Gnome pattern
- 1.5cm (½in) wide strips of paper in pinkish red, purple/white pattern, purple and origami red/white design
- Paper: 6 × 4cm (2¼ × 1½in) pinkish red for hat and arms; 3 × 3cm (1¼ × 1¼in) light pink for face; 2 × 6cm (¾ × 2¼in) purple for slippers and 1 × 2cm (½ × ¾in) black for bow tie
- Holographic paper (pink)
- Text sticker
- Corner scissors (regal)

Decorate with text sticker and bow tie.

4 The house gnome's bucket with tulips

- Card: 8.9 × 6.4cm (3½ × 2½in) pink and 8 × 5.5cm (3¼ × 2¾in) white
- Bucket pattern
- 1.5cm (½in) wide strips of paper in pink, pink pattern, purple and purple pattern
- Paper: 2 × 6cm (¾ × 2¼in) pink flamed for tulips; 2 × 6cm (¾ × 2¼in) green for leaves
- Holographic paper (pink)
- Tulip and leaf patterns

Note: the dotted lines are the fold lines.

Cover section 1a and then 1b each with a strip of pink paper. Decorate with cut-out tulips and leaves, or cut the flowers out of a garden magazine!

5 The forest gnome's bucket with little trees

- Card: 8.9 × 6.4cm (3½ × 2½in) spring green and 8 × 5.5cm (3¼ × 2¾in) white
- Bucket pattern
- 1.5cm (½in) wide strips of paper in green, dark brown pattern, light green and light brown pattern
- Paper: 4 × 6cm (1½ × 2¼in) green/brown for twigs; 2 × 2cm (¾ × ¾in) light brown for rabbit
- Holographic paper (gold)
- Punch (twig)
- Punch (rabbit)

6 The garden gnome's bucket with frogs

- Card: 8.9 × 6.4cm (3½ × 2½in) yellow and 8 × 5.5cm (3¼ × 2¾in) white
- Bucket pattern
- 1.5cm (½in) wide strips of paper in red, green pattern and yellow
- Paper: 2 × 4cm (¾ × 1½in) red for handle; green for the frogs
- Holographic paper (green)
- Punch (frog)

Decorate with handle and frog.

Horse and chestnut

The horse is made following the instructions for card 1 and the chestnut following those for card 2.

Card 1

- Card: 13 × 26cm (5 × 10¼in) dark red, 10 × 10.5cm (4 × 4¼in) red and 9.4 × 9.8cm (3¾ × 3¾in) white
- Paper: red castles pattern, 12 × 12cm (4¾ × 4¾in)
- Horse pattern
- 2cm (¾in) wide strips of paper in the following colours: black and white pattern, black, grey and speckled grey
- Paper: 4 × 3cm (1½ × 1¼in) black/white pattern for front legs; 4 × 4cm (1½ × 1½in) black for hind legs and tail; 3 × 4cm (1¼ × 1½in) grey for head
- Holographic paper (silver)
- Black fine-liner pen

Cut the numbered part out of the card. Trace the head, legs and tail on to appropriate paper, cut out and attach. Draw the eye.

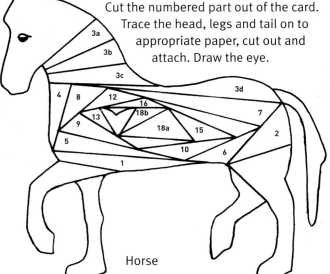

Horse

Card 2

- Card: 13 × 26cm (5 × 10¼in) mustard yellow P48, 11.5 × 11.5cm (4½ × 4½in) rust and 11 × 11cm (4¼ × 4¼in) caramel
- Chestnut pattern
- 2cm (¾in) wide strips of origami paper in brown, salmon, gold, striped, and flower pattern
- Grey-brown pattern paper, 9 × 8cm (3½ × 3¼in) for husk
- Holographic paper (mother-of-pearl)
- Animal sticker

Cut only the numbered oval shape out of the caramel coloured card. After the iris folding, trace the husk on to the grey-brown paper, cut out, including all the thorns, and attach to the front of the card. Decorate with an animal sticker.

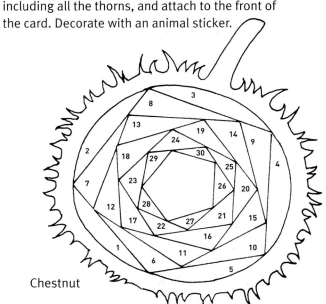

Chestnut

Card 3

- Card: 14 × 28cm (5½ × 11in) sepia, 13 × 13cm (5 × 5in) brown and 11 × 11cm (4¼ × 4¼in) white
- Horse pattern
- 2cm (¾in) wide strips of paper in the following colours: dark brown, mid brown, light brown and 'scratched' brown
- Paper: 4 × 3cm (1½ × 1¼in) dark brown for front legs; 4 × 4cm (1½ × 1½in) mid brown for hind legs; 3 × 4cm (1¼ × 1½in) light brown for head; 4 × 2cm (1½ × ¾in) 'scratched' brown for tail
- Holographic paper (gold)
- Sticker edges (gold)
- Black fine-liner pen

Decorate the card with sticker edges and a rosette.

Card 4

- Card: 13 × 26cm (5 × 10¼in) green, 11.8 × 11.8cm (4¾ × 4¾in) bright green and 11.3 × 11.3cm (4½ × 4½in) beige
- Chestnut pattern
- 2cm (¾in) wide strips of paper in five different shades of green
- Fresh green paper, 9 × 8cm (3½ × 3¼in) for husk
- Holographic paper (gold)
- Stickers

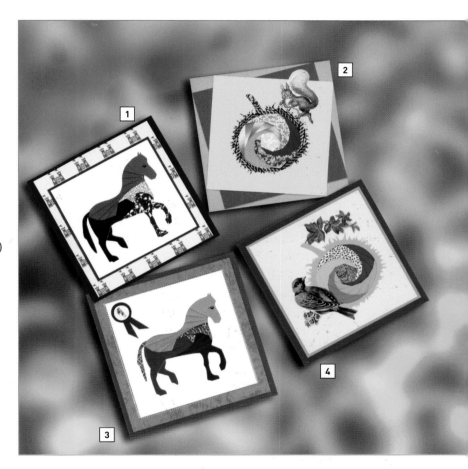

Jam jar and pot

The jam jar is made following the instructions for card 1, the pot using those for card 2.

1 Marmalade

- Card: 14.8 × 21cm (5¾ × 8¼in) orange and 11 × 8cm (4¼ × 3¼in) white
- Paper: blossom pattern, 14.8 × 8cm (5¾ × 3¼in)
- Jam jar pattern
- 2cm (¾in) wide strips of paper in orange with stripes, bright orange, orange with dots and light orange
- 1cm (½in) wide strips of gold paper
- Holographic paper (gold)
- Small oranges stickers

Sections 2, 6, etc. and 4, 8, etc. are filled in with two strips each, one orange, one gold. In each section, make sure the orange strip is against the dotted line, and then attach. Put a small folded strip of gold on top of the orange strip, along the fold line, and attach. Open the card out during the iris folding to check that the edges are in the right place. Attach the small oranges stickers.

2 Stew

- Card: 13 × 26cm (5 × 10¼in) rust colour and 10.6 × 9cm (4¼ × 3½in) white
- Paper: green pattern, 12.5 × 12.5cm (5 × 5in) and orange, 11 × 9.4cm (4¼ × 3¾in)
- Pot pattern
- 2cm (¾in) wide strips of paper in dark green pattern, brown, orange and green pattern
- Brown paper, 5 × 7cm (2 × 2¾in) for lid and handle
- Holographic paper (orange)
- Gold decorative sticker

After the iris folding, cut out the lid and handle and attach. Add the decoration. Attach the white card to the orange card, add these to the green patterned paper and attach to double card.

3 Soup

- Card: 13 × 26cm (5 × 10¼in) mustard yellow P48, 11.5 × 11.5cm (4½ × 4½in) yellow pattern and 9.5 × 9.5cm (3¾ × 3¾in) white
- Dark brown paper, 12 × 12cm (4¾ × 4¾in)
- Pot pattern
- 2cm (¾in) wide strips of paper in dark brown, yellow, rust colour and gold spotted
- Dark brown paper, 2.5 × 5cm (1 × 2in) for lid
- Holographic paper (bronze)
- Stickers (gold dots)

Cut the soup ladle out of the holographic paper and attach.

4 Cooking pears

- Card: 13 × 26cm (5 × 10¼in) Christmas red P43 and 10 × 9cm (4 × 3½in) white
- Parchment paper with wavy red pattern, 11.5 × 11.5cm (4½ × 4½in)
- Pot pattern
- 2cm (¾in) wide strips of paper in burgundy, brown with 'scratches', yellow and violet
- Brown paper with 'scratches', 2.5 × 5cm (1 × 2in) for lid
- Holographic paper (burgundy)
- Gold decorative sticker
- Four small yellow paper fasteners

After the iris folding, cut out the half pears and the lid and attach them. Add decoration. Using the paper fasteners, attach the parchment paper to the front of the double red card. Attach the white card to the background.

5 Tomato chutney

- Card: 14.8 × 21cm (5¾ × 8¼in) green diamond pattern, 12 × 8cm (4¾ × 3¼in) red and 11 × 7cm (4¼ × 2¾in) white
- Jam jar pattern
- 2cm (¾in) wide strips of paper in light green, rose pattern, plain red and green with stripes
- Holographic paper (red)
- Red diamond paper, 1.5 × 5cm (½ × 2in), for lid
- Red yarn

6 Blackberry jam

- Card: 14.8 × 21cm (5¾ × 8¼in) violet, 11 × 10.5cm (4¼ × 4¼in) blackberry P185 and 11 × 7cm (4¼ × 2¾in) white
- Origami paper lilac design 11 × 7cm (4¼ × 2¾in)
- Jam jar pattern
- 2cm (¾in) wide strips of paper in purple, old rose, purple dotted and violet shine
- Holographic paper (purple)

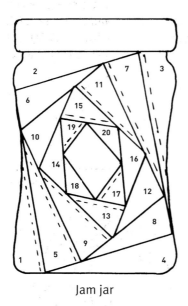

Jam jar

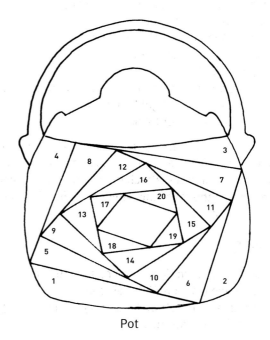

Pot

Scent bottles and spherical candle

The scent bottle is made using the instructions for cards 1 and 2, the candle using those for card 3.

Card 1

- Card: 14 × 28cm (5¾ × 8¼in) green, 13.3 × 13.3cm (5¼ × 5¼in) violet and 10.5 × 7.5cm (4¼ × 3in) white
- Floral pattern paper, 12.5 × 12.5cm (5 × 5in)
- Scent bottle pattern 1
- 1.5cm (½in) wide strips of paper in the following colours: pink striped, two floral designs and violet
- Paper: 3 × 3.5cm (1¼ × 1½in) violet for cap; and 1 × 2cm (½ × ¾in) gold for neck
- Holographic paper (pink)

Cut only the numbered part of the pattern out of the white card. After the iris folding, cut out the neck, cap and a flower and attach them. On double green card, attach the following: violet card, floral paper and the white card.

Card 2

- Card: 14 × 28cm (5¾ × 8¼in) sea green and 11 × 11cm (4¼ × 4¼in) grey-blue
- Sea green/pink striped paper, 13 × 13cm (5 × 5in)
- Scent bottle pattern 2

- 2cm (¾in) wide strips of paper in the following colours: green, green striped, blue and mottled light blue

Cut only the square out of the back of the blue-grey card. After the iris folding, cut a straight line of about 2cm (¾in) across each corner, and also a strip of width 0.5cm (¼in). Now attach the sheet of striped paper to the front of the double sea-green card. Attach the blue-grey card and stick on the triangles at each corner, at a distance of 0.5cm (¼in). Cut the cap out of the mottled light blue paper and attach.

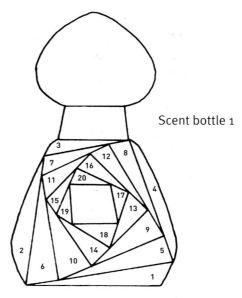

Scent bottle 1

Card 3

- Card: 13 × 26cm (5 × 10¼in) Christmas red, 12 × 12cm (4¾ × 4¾in) gold design, 10.5 × 9.5cm (4¼ × 3¾in) red and 10 × 9cm (4 × 3½in) ivory white
- Candle pattern
- 1.5cm (½in) wide strips of paper in the following colours: burgundy, gold pattern, dark red pattern, gold, beige/red pattern
- Gold paper, 4 × 3cm (1½ × 1¼in) for flame
- Holographic paper (flame red)

Cut the candle out of the ivory white card and fill it in with strips. Cut out the golden flame and attach. Attach the white card to the red card, then to the gold card and finally to the double Christmas red card.

Card 4

- Card: 14.8 × 21cm (5¾ × 8¼in) dark red and 11 × 7.5cm (4 × 3¼in) pink
- Paper: 13.5 × 8.8cm (5¼ × 3½in) salmon, 12 × 8cm (4¾ × 3¼in) dark pink and 10.5 × 7cm (4¼ × 2¾in) floral design
- Scent bottle pattern 1
- 1.5cm (½in) wide strips of paper in the following colours: green pattern, salmon, pink striped design and light yellow
- Holographic paper (salmon)
- Paper: 3 × 3.5cm (1¼ × 1½in) light yellow for cap and 1 × 2cm (½ × ¾in) dark pink for neck

Begin by attaching the floral design paper to the pink card.

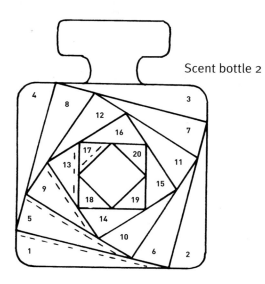

Scent bottle 2

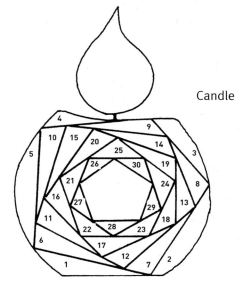

Candle

Card 5

- Card: 14 × 28cm (5½ × 11in) sky blue, 12 × 11.5cm (4¾ × 4¼in) blue-green and 10 × 8.5cm (4 × 3¼in) white
- Scent bottle 2 pattern
- 2cm (¾in) wide strips of paper in the following colours: blue, blue/white pattern, petrol and blue-green
- 1cm (½in) wide strips of silver paper
- Holographic paper (blue)

Note: squares 1, 5, 9, 13 and 17 each get a blue strip up to the dotted line and directly on top of that a small strip of silver up to the fold line (see page 90, card 1, Marmalade). Decorate the left-hand side of the card with 14 × 1cm (5½ × ½in) strips of blue pattern paper and petrol-coloured paper.

Card 6

- Card: 14.8 × 21cm (5¾ × 8¼in) light green and 10.5 × 8cm (4¼ × 3¼in) green
- Green paper with white floral design, 13.5 × 9cm (5¼ × 3½in)
- Candle pattern
- 1.5cm (½in) wide strips of paper in the following colours: moss green, green and white pattern, yellow-green design, light green and silver
- Holographic paper (silver)
- Silver paper, 4 × 3cm (1½ × 1¼in), for flame

Acknowledgements

With thanks to: Kars & Co B.V.
Pergamano International
Pipoos
Damen Papier Royaal
Papicolor International
Em-Je B.V.